THE DEBBIE THROWER
CHRISTMAS HANDBOOK

DEBBIE THROWER
EDITED BY CAROLINE PLAISTED

BBC BOOKS

This book is published to accompany *The Debbie Thrower Show* broadcast every weekday on BBC Radio 2.

Published by BBC Books,
an imprint of BBC Worldwide Publishing,
BBC Worldwide Limited, Woodlands,
80 Wood Lane, London W12 0TT.

First published 1997
ISBN 0 563 38342 9

Edited by Caroline Plaisted
Designed by Judith Robertson
Line illustrations by Kate Simunek
Photographs by Juliet Piddington
Styling by Marian Price
Home Economist: Sarah Ramsbottom

Set in Bembo
Printed by Martins the Printers Ltd, Berwick-upon-Tweed
Bound by Hunter & Foulis Ltd, Edinburgh
Colour separations by Radstock Reproductions Ltd, Midsomer Norton
Colour printed by Lawrence Allen Ltd, Weston-super-Mare
Cover printed by Belmont Press, Northampton

CONTENTS

I would like to thank Bridget Apps,
the former editor of *The Debbie Thrower Show*
for all her help, common sense, and unfailing
good humour during the compiling
of this book

INTRODUCTION

There's a well-worn saying in my family that 'time spent in reconnaissance is seldom wasted', and it's true that good planning is the key to a great Christmas. However, you don't need to plan your campaign with military precision as, with the help of this book, you should be able to enjoy Christmas as well. Within these pages you'll find everything you need to create the perfect Christmas - if such a thing exists.

It's tempting for us to hark back to childhood Christmases and think that things were enviably simpler then. My own were spent in Devon some six miles from the sea and Christmas week began for us when, armed with secateurs, we went on forays to pick holly and mistletoe.

While the rest of my family must have been busy in the kitchen, I have vivid memories of carol singing around the village and meeting the evening trains at the local railway station, seeing weary travellers climbing off bemused (and I hope amused) to find fresh-faced singers serenading their arrival.

Christmas Day itself dawned with that wonderful heavyweight of a stocking at the end of the bed. Family presents were opened after Holy Communion in the packed parish church. I recall the rest of the day as a haze of good food, candlelight, laughter and games. What this reverie teaches me now is that no effort we make is ever wasted at this time of year. Rather, we should think of it as an investment in the memories of those younger than ourselves.

But let me strike a practical note again and repeat that we can only do so much. Few among us have time to do all we might wish for Christmas from scratch. As you know, on *The Debbie Thrower Show*, we plan for Christmas by inviting along a host of people expert in the various aspects of preparing for the festivities. We've decided to give you the chance to invite these oracles permanently into your home by including their experience and advice in this book.

Mary Berry shares with us her ideas for both traditional and more unusual Christmas cakes, biscuits and puddings. Nadine Abensur is here to help you cater for any vegetarians in the family. For those with the opportunity and energy, Kevin Woodford gives us recipes for a festive supper party. The sweet-toothed among you will surely be tempted by Chris Walker's Radio 2 Christmas Truffle Collection, and you can enjoy stress-free party planning with his canapés and party food suggestions.

My own family recipes for the traditional Christmas lunch are here and, just in case you have any leftover turkey, Pat Chapman has dishes to inspire the cook and your family's palates. Fiona Hunter of the Good Housekeeping Institute gives us important advice on food hygiene, which is obviously vital at a time when our fridges are overloaded with cooked and uncooked food. Delia Smith and Simon Hopkinson have kindly given us their expert culinary tips, which you will find throughout the book. And if you are wondering what to drink with all that food, Martin Ward is here to guide you.

When it comes to Christmas, we all love to exchange appropriate gifts, but the thought of the epic task of finding them can be daunting. So we've asked Sally O'Sullivan to help your 'fingers do the walking' with some ingenious mail-order ideas. And Stephanie Donaldson has contributed her recipes for wonderfully aromatic gifts and decorations. Adam Pasco has tackled the ever-present evergreen problem: Christmas trees without needle-drop, and gives advice on keeping your houseplants at their healthiest during the festive season. So make the most of your personal experts, courtesy of *The Debbie Thrower Show*: it is their job to perfect the menus, choose the wines, invent novel decorations to make, and generally dot the 'i's and cross the 't's when it comes to lists of what not to forget.

I knew we were on the right track with this book when I mentioned on air what we were up to. By return of post, we received many letters of encouragement and anticipation from our listeners. Thank you to all of you who have been kind enough to send in your own recipes and suggestions for preparing for Christmas, many of which are included. All of us on the Show have had great fun putting it all together – and now it's over to you.

Have a very merry Christmas,

Debbie Thrower

THE CHRISTMAS YEAR

Each year I say to myself, 'I must do things earlier next Christmas,' but I know all too well how quickly that promise gets forgotten! Among the wonderful letters I have received from listeners to the programme, I have been given many useful tips, and I offer these, along with a few of my own, in this 12-month calendar of ideas, which should help you to spread the load - *and* not forget anything.

JANUARY

- ☐ Write thank you letters.
- ☐ 6 January - take down decorations.
- ☐ Recycle your tree (see page 80).
- ☐ Recycle your cards, and the bottles and tins from all the festivities.
- ☐ Exchange unsuitable gifts.
- ☐ Buy bargain gifts for next Christmas in the sales.

APRIL/MAY

- ☐ Start saving jars and bottles for making jams and pickles later in the year.
- ☐ Follow Adam Pasco's plant advice on page 72.

JUNE/JULY/AUGUST

- ☐ Seek out non-seasonal presents in the sales and on holiday.
- ☐ Buy your Christmas booze duty-free.
- ☐ Make jams and bottled fruits ready for December.
- ☐ Follow Adam Pasco's plant advice on page 72.

SEPTEMBER

- ☐ Write your Christmas Present List - see page 136.
- ☐ Do your mail order shopping - see page 89.
- ☐ Check last posting dates - see page 138.
- ☐ Buy or order your cards.
- ☐ Ascertain your family's Christmas arrangements - who's going where?
- ☐ Buy your cake and pudding ingredients.
- ☐ Make your Christmas pickles.
- ☐ Follow Adam Pasco's plant advice on page 72.

OCTOBER

- ☐ Make mincemeat - see page 48.
- ☐ Invite any Christmas Day guests.
- ☐ Chase up mail order presents.
- ☐ Bake your cake and puddings.
- ☐ Hire any extra equipment you need for children and elderly relatives - see page 129.
- ☐ Start buying the presents.
- ☐ Follow Adam Pasco's plant advice on page 72.
- ☐ Arrange for Christmas-gift pictures to be framed now.

NOVEMBER

- ☐ Write your food list - see page 130.
- ☐ Buy foods that will freeze or store.
- ☐ Buy more presents.
- ☐ Order your fresh turkey.
- ☐ Start freezing ice cubes.
- ☐ Order extra glasses from your off-licence.
- ☐ Freeze slices of lemon (wipe them 'dry' and freeze them on a baking tray before transferring to sealed freezer bags) ready for Christmas drinks.
- ☐ Buy your postage stamps.
- ☐ Write your cards.
- ☐ Feed your cake - see page 14.
- ☐ Make Stephanie Donaldson's gifts and aromatic delights.

EARLY DECEMBER

- ☐ Finish writing cards and post second-class - see page 132.
- ☐ Wrap and tag your gifts - see page 136.
- ☐ Distribute and post presents.
- ☐ Hang your own cards as you receive them.
- ☐ Order Christmas flowers.
- ☐ Check you have everything to get you through the school holidays.
- ☐ Reserve your tree.
- ☐ Fill in your Emergency Names and Numbers on page 141.

MID-DECEMBER

- ☐ Have you done everything in the October and November lists above?
- ☐ Double-check your food shopping lists.
- ☐ Distribute and deliver any local cards and presents.
- ☐ Your Christmas Week Countdown is on page 126.

Have fun and enjoy!

MARY BERRY'S CHRISTMAS BAKING

Mary Berry, author of more than 25 cookery books, is well known to listeners of *The Debbie Thrower Show* as our very own cookery expert. Mary has been broadcasting her Christmas cookery advice for us for the last three years, and here she shares with us her expertise in Christmas baking and icing.

COOKER CONSIDERATIONS

A recent conversation with Mary Berry made me realize that we needed to remind you that no two ovens perform alike - not even two of the same make. That's why you will find that the recipes we've included in this book say 'bake for about so many minutes' or 'until the cake is golden brown'. Mary has passed on a few things you should consider about your own cooker:

If you have a fan or convection oven it will, as a general rule, be about 20-25 per cent hotter than a conventional oven; because the air is circulating, the cooking will also be faster.

With a fan oven you can start a recipe from cold, as it heats up so quickly. With recipes that have a cooking time longer than 30 minutes, there is probably no need to pre-heat a fan oven. Cover food with foil to prevent it over-browning.

If you cook with an Aga, you can lower the heat of the roasting oven for baking by slotting the cold plain shelf provided with your Aga above the food. This will lower the temperature below the shelf to a baking temperature for 20 minutes or so.

Whatever type of cooker you have, the more foods you cook at the same time, the longer they will take, as the temperature of the oven is reduced.

Buy an oven thermometer and check the heat of your oven. This will help you get any timings right.

Because your own oven's cooking time may be at variance with the guides given in our recipes, try to avoid cake baking in particular when you are in a hurry. Having gone to the effort of mixing your Christmas cake, we'd hate to think of you battling with burnt offerings or suffering with a cake that has sunk in the middle!

VICTORIANA CHRISTMAS CAKE

MAKES 1 20 CM (8 IN) ROUND CAKE

INGREDIENTS

550 g (1¼ lb) mixed dried fruit, including peel
100 g (4 oz) raisins, chopped if large
100 g (4 oz) currants
100 g (4 oz) glacé cherries, quartered
150 ml (5 fl oz) medium-sweet or sweet sherry
175 g (6 oz) soft baking margarine
175 g (6 oz) light brown muscovado sugar
zest of 1 lemon
zest of 1 orange
3 large eggs
1 tablespoon black treacle
50 g (2 oz) blanched almonds, chopped
100 g (4 oz) plain flour
50 g (2 oz) self-raising flour
1 level teaspoon mixed spice

YOU WILL NEED

2 mixing bowls
20 cm (8 in) round cake tin
silicone paper or baking parchment
sieve
foil
skewer

THIS IS AN EASY, *different and special cake. The fruit is soaked for several days in sherry, which makes it very moist. This is not a really deep cake so do not expect it to rise to the top of the tin. Baking times can vary according to your own individual oven - please refer to page 9 for guidance.*

Put the dried fruit and cherries in a bowl, pour over the sherry, cover with a lid and leave to soak for at least 3 days, stirring daily.

Pre-heat the oven to 300°F/150°C/gas 2 and grease and line the cake tin with the silicone paper or baking parchment.

Put the margarine, sugar, lemon and orange zest, eggs, treacle and almonds in a large bowl. Sift together the flours and mixed spice and then add these to the bowl. Mix together until evenly blended, then stir in the soaked fruit and sherry. Spoon the mixture into the tin and smooth the top flat. Bake in the oven for 2 hours, then reduce the heat to 275°F/140°C/gas 1 and bake for a further 1¼ hours. (If the cake seems to be getting too brown on top, cover it with a sheet of foil.)

Test with a warm skewer to see if the cake is done. If the skewer comes out clean when inserted in the centre of the cake, it is cooked. If not, bake for a further 15 minutes before checking again. Leave to cool completely in the tin.

AMERICAN LIGHT CHRISTMAS CAKE

MAKES 1 23 CM (9 IN) ROUND CAKE

INGREDIENTS

350 g (12 oz) glacé cherries
225 g (8 oz) can pineapple
in natural juice
350 g (12 oz) ready-to-eat
dried apricots
100 g (4 oz) whole
blanched almonds
zest of 2 lemons
350 g (12 oz) sultanas
250 g (9 oz) self-raising
flour
250 g (9 oz) caster sugar
250 g (9 oz) soft baking
margarine
75 g (3 oz) ground almonds
5 medium eggs

TO DECORATE
whole blanched almonds
glacé cherries, halved
glacé pineapple, in pieces

TO FINISH
100 g (4 oz) icing sugar,
sifted

YOU WILL NEED

deep 23 cm (9 in) round
cake tin
silicone paper or baking
parchment
2 mixing bowls
foil
skewer

UNLIKE TRADITIONAL Christmas cakes, this mixture produces a light, succulent and moist cake.

PRE-HEAT THE OVEN TO 325°F/160°C/GAS 3. GREASE AND DOUBLE-LINE THE CAKE TIN.

Cut the cherries into quarters, rinse and drain them well. Drain and roughly chop the pineapple, then dry both the cherries and pineapple very thoroughly on kitchen paper. Snip the apricots into pieces. Roughly chop the almonds. Place the prepared fruit and nuts in a mixing bowl with the lemon zest and sultanas and mix them together gently. Place the remaining ingredients in another mixing bowl and beat well for 1 minute until smooth. Lightly fold in the fruit and nuts and then turn the mixture into the prepared cake tin. Level the surface and decorate the top with the almonds, cherries and pineapple.

Bake the cake in the pre-heated oven for about 2¼ hours or until golden brown. After 1 hour, cover the cake loosely with foil to prevent the top becoming too dark in colour. Test with a warm skewer to see if the cake is done - insert it into the centre of the cake, and it should come out clean. Leave the cake to cool in the tin for about 30 minutes before turning it out to cool completely on a wire rack.

When you are ready, mix the icing sugar with a little water and drizzle this over the cake to glaze.

ALMOND PASTE

SUFFICIENT TO COVER A 20 CM (8 IN) ROUND CAKE

INGREDIENTS

175 g (6 oz) icing sugar
175 g (6 oz) ground
  almonds
175 g (6 oz) caster sugar
3 large egg yolks, beaten
almond essence
juice of half a lemon
apricot jam, warmed

YOU WILL NEED

sieve
mixing bowl
silicone paper or baking
  parchment
pencil
scissors
rolling pin
pastry brush
palette knife
smooth-sided, high, round
  cake tin

ALTHOUGH THERE ARE some very good ready-made almond pastes available from supermarkets these days, I really do recommend that you make your own if you have the time. You will thank yourself for making the effort when you taste it.

Sift the icing sugar into a mixing bowl, add the ground almonds and sugar and mix well.

Add the egg yolks, and flavour to taste, first with the almond essence and then with the lemon juice. Work the mixture into a small smooth ball by hand – but do not over-knead.

There are two ways I recommend to cover a cake.

For a clean-cut, professional appearance: Divide the almond paste into 2 pieces, one using two-thirds of the paste, the other using one-third. Cut out in greaseproof paper a circle to fit the top of the cake and a strip to fit around the side. Lay these out on the table and sugar them with a little caster sugar. Roll out the smaller piece of almond paste to fit the circle and the large piece to fit the strip generously. For the sides, it helps to roll a long sausage shape of almond paste, and then to flatten it.

Brush the top of the cake with the warmed apricot jam, then put the circle of almond paste in position, leaving the paper on. Turn the cake over. Brush the side of the cake with jam and fix the strip of almond paste to the side and remove the paper.

Neaten the edges with a palette knife and roll a straight-sided empty round cake tin around the cake to make the side smooth. Turn the cake back to the right way up and put it on a board. Level the top with a rolling pin.

For a softer edge and a 'fast finish' covering: First, brush the top of the cake with the warmed apricot jam, then roll out the almond paste in one large round piece and cover the cake, smoothing down the sides with your hands.

When you have finished, cover the cake with greaseproof paper and place it in an airtight cake tin. Keep this in a cool place for 5-7 days to allow the almond paste to dry before you ice the cake.

ROYAL ICING

SUFFICIENT TO COVER A 20 CM (8 IN) ROUND CAKE

INGREDIENTS

675 g (1½ lb) icing sugar
4 egg whites
3 teaspoons lemon juice
1½ teaspoon glycerine

YOU WILL NEED

sieve
whisk
2 mixing bowls

THIS IS A TRADITIONAL, *melt-in-the-mouth icing. Don't forget that you should wait about a week for the almond paste to dry a little before you ice your cake.*

Sieve the icing sugar into a bowl. In a separate bowl, whisk the 3 egg whites until they become frothy. Add the icing sugar, a spoonful at a time. Then add the lemon juice and glycerine. Beat the icing until it is very stiff and white and will stand up in peaks.

Now refer to the icing instructions given on page 14 and then store as directed.

ICING AND STORING YOUR CHRISTMAS CAKE

After baking, wrap your cake in a double thickness of baking parchment, greaseproof paper or tin foil before keeping it in an airtight cake tin or container. My family prefers the cake to be a little 'boozy', so I make tiny holes in the top of the cake with a fine clean skewer or needle and then spoon a small amount of brandy over the top. I do this at weekly intervals up until the time that I cover it with almond paste and leave the paste to dry before icing.

To make a snow scene finish, thin down half of the Royal Icing recipe (see page 13) with a little egg white. Mix this to a spreading consistency and, with a palette knife, spread it over the top of the almond-pasted cake to give a smooth surface. Put the remaining icing around the sides of the cake and, using a fork, spike up the icing to form rough peaks of 'snow'. Now decorate the cake with your traditional family decorations. Or you could keep a little of the icing covered in a cup and then, next day, use it to fix a candle to the centre of the cake. Alternatively, tie a large red, gold or tartan ribbon around the cake as if it was a parcel, finishing with a bow in the front.

I know that some people prefer their cake to be iced with fondant icing. This is a real fiddle to make and, as there are many excellent ready-made versions available from supermarkets, I haven't given a recipe here. When you come to ice your cake with it, be sure to roll the fondant icing on a clean, flat surface: marble is perfect but a pastry board will do. Ensure that your hands and the rolling pin are very clean, as the white icing will stain easily. Use icing sugar or cornflour on the board and rolling pin to prevent the icing from sticking, but take care not to allow it to get too dry, as it will crack when you are rolling it out.

Before applying the fondant icing, cover the almond paste with warmed apricot jam. Make templates as you did for covering the cake with the almond paste (see page 12) and cover with the fondant icing by the same method.

Always store your cake in an airtight cake tin, in a cool place, until you are ready to eat it.

MINCEMEAT STREUSEL

SERVES 16

INGREDIENTS

FOR THE PASTRY BASE
175 g (6 oz) flour
100 g (4 oz) butter
1½ tablespoons icing sugar
a little cold water

FOR THE FILLING
450 g (1 lb) good-quality mincemeat

FOR THE TOPPING
75 g (3 oz) margarine, just melted
75 g (3 oz) self-raising flour
40 g (1½ oz) semolina
40 g (1½ oz) caster sugar

TO DECORATE
icing sugar, sifted

YOU WILL NEED

18 x 28 cm (7 x 11 in) swiss-roll tin
mixing bowl
cling film
coarse grater

A DIFFERENT AND *easier way of making mince pie. The attractive topping makes it less heavy, and as a bonus you get plenty of mincemeat in each slice!*

PRE-HEAT THE OVEN TO 400°F/200°C/GAS 6. LIGHTLY GREASE THE SWISS-ROLL TIN.

First make the thin pastry base. Measure the flour into a bowl and rub in the butter until the mixture resembles fine breadcrumbs. Stir in the sugar and sufficient water to mix to a firm dough. Wrap the mixture in the cling film and chill it in the refrigerator for about half an hour. Then roll out the dough on a lightly floured surface and use it to line the tin. Spread it generously with the mincemeat.

For the topping, measure all the ingredients into a bowl and mix them together to form a soft dough. Using a coarse grater, grate this mixture on top of the mincemeat. If it is too soft to grate, then chill it in the refrigerator for about 15 minutes before trying again.

Cook the streusel in the pre-heated oven for about 20-30 minutes, turning once during the cooking if necessary: it should be a pale golden brown when it is ready. Allow it to cool before dividing into slices and dusting with icing sugar to serve.

BYRE FARM CHRISTMAS PUDDING

SERVES 6-8

INGREDIENTS

175 g (6 oz) raisins
75 g (3 oz) currants
75 g (3 oz) sultanas
50 g (2 oz) candied peel,
  chopped
50 g (2 oz) shelled mixed
  nuts, chopped
75 g (3 oz) self-raising
  flour
2 medium eggs
100 g (4 oz) fresh white
  breadcrumbs
100 g (4 oz) shredded suet
150 ml (5 fl oz) stout
1 cooking apple, peeled,
  cored and diced
zest and juice of 1 orange
zest and juice of 1 lemon
2 tablespoons black treacle
½ teaspoon nutmeg
½ teaspoon mixed spice

YOU WILL NEED

mixing bowl
1.2 litre (2 pint) pudding
  basin
greaseproof paper
tin foil
string
large pan

IT IS NOT A *mistake that this recipe does not include sugar in its ingredients. As most people serve brandy butter or cream with the pudding, you should find that it is perfectly sweet enough. However, if you prefer, add 50 g (2 oz) of caster sugar to the ingredients.*

You can make this pudding at least three months ahead, as long as you have a cool larder or enough space in your fridge for storage. Or to freeze the pudding, turn it out after it has cooled, wrap it in baking parchment, then an outer layer of foil, and freeze. Thaw completely on Christmas Eve, then simply return it to its bowl and simmer for an hour on Christmas Day.

Place all the ingredients in a large mixing bowl and mix together very thoroughly. Turn the mixture into the greased pudding basin, cover with a lid made of greased greaseproof paper and foil, secured with string, and simmer in a pan of boiling water, covered, for 8 hours. The water should reach half-way up the sides of the pudding basin, and may need topping up during cooking. Remove from the pan, cool and cover with a fresh piece of foil to store.

On Christmas Day, cover with clean foil, secured with string, and simmer in a covered pan of boiling water for 1 hour, then turn out and serve hot with brandy butter or Brandy Cream (see page 17).

BRANDY CREAM

INGREDIENTS

*150 ml (5 fl oz) double
cream
1 tablespoon caster sugar
2 tablespoons brandy*

YOU WILL NEED

*mixing bowl
whisk*

S IMPLE AND DELICIOUS, *this can be made a couple of days ahead and stored, covered, in the refrigerator.*

Measure the ingredients into a bowl, whisk until thick and soft peaks form. Turn the Brandy Cream into a bowl and serve with Byre Farm Christmas Pudding.

LISTENER'S RECIPE

INGREDIENTS

*2 cinnamon sticks
3 blades mace
4 cloves
1 teaspoon grated
nutmeg
2 tablespoons sugar
1 bottle red wine
1.5 litres (2½ pints)
lemonade
3 oranges, sliced
1 lemon, sliced*

MULLED WINE

W HEN I MENTIONED *to listeners that I was looking for Christmas recipes the letters flooded in. It has been a hard task to select the best but you will find them scattered throughout the book. Many thanks to all who took the trouble and care to write in to me. Recipes for mulled wine were very popular and this is from Gill Allanson in Wirral.*

Simmer all the ingredients together in a large pan for 15 minutes, being careful not to let it boil. Serve the mulled wine warm. If not using immediately, strain off the spices and fruit and keep the cooled wine in a bottle in the fridge. You can store it for a few days, warming up a glass or two as required.

CHRISTMAS BRANDY ICE-CREAM PUDDING

SERVES 8

INGREDIENTS

FOR THE ICE-CREAM
50 g (2 oz) dried cranberries
50 g (2 oz) dried apricots,
chopped
50 g (2 oz) raisins
3 tablespoons brandy
4 large eggs, separated
100 g (4 oz) caster sugar
300 ml (½ pint) double
cream, lightly whipped

FOR THE BRANDY FRUIT
TOPPING
6 tablespoons water
100 g (4 oz) caster sugar
25 g (1 oz) dried
cranberries
25 g (1 oz) dried apricots,
chopped
25 g (1 oz) raisins
2 tablespoons brandy

TO DECORATE
a sprig of holly

YOU WILL NEED

small bowl
plate or cling film
electric whisk
1.75 litre (3 pint) pudding
basin
small pan
(Cont. opposite)

YOU DON'T NEED *an ice-cream maker for this recipe as there is no re-whipping. This pudding is rich and creamy, loaded with fruits and rather boozy! Dried cranberries are a fairly new ingredient, they're rather like dried apricots, and you should be able to find them in good supermarkets.*

First soak the cranberries, apricots and raisins in the brandy for at least 6 hours. Do this in the small bowl and cover with the plate or cling film. After 6 hours, most of the brandy will be absorbed into the fruit.

Now make the ice-cream. Start by making a meringue with the egg whites: whisk the whites with an electric whisk on full speed until they look like cloud. Then whisk in the caster sugar a teaspoon at a time, still at full speed, until all the sugar has been included. Fold in the egg yolks and the cream. Lastly fold in the soaked fruit. Turn into the pudding basin, cover it and freeze.

To make the topping, measure the water and sugar into a small pan. Stir over a low heat until the sugar has dissolved then boil the syrup for 1 minute. Cool a little. Put the second lot of fruit into the jam jar, pour over the syrup, add the brandy, stir, and cover with a lid and store on the larder shelf until needed at Christmas. Should the syrup crystallize, gently reheat it until the crystals disappear, if necessary adding a little water.

350 g (12 oz) clean jam jar
serving plate
bowl larger than the pudding
basin (for when you are
due to serve)

To serve, dip the pudding basin into another bigger bowl of very hot water for a moment. Invert the serving plate and position this on top of the pudding basin before immediately turning it the right way up. The ice-cream now needs to be covered with cling film and returned to the freezer until 15 minutes before serving time. Then decorate it with a sprig of holly.

Serve the pudding in wedges and spoon over a little of the cold fruit brandy sauce.

LISTENER'S RECIPE

GINGERBREAD SHAPES

INGREDIENTS

100 g (4 oz) soft baking
margarine
225 g (8 oz) flour
100 g (4 oz) soft brown
sugar
1 teaspoon ground
ginger
1 tablespoon black
treacle
1 tablespoon golden
syrup
1 teaspoon orange juice

T HIS FESTIVE RECIPE *is from Maureen Martin in Sunbury.*

PRE-HEAT THE OVEN TO 350°F/180°F/GAS 4.

In a bowl, rub the margarine into the flour and then add all the other ingredients. Mix them together well. Now roll out the dough on a floured board and cut it into Christmas shapes (holly, trees and bells are best.)

Put the shapes onto the baking tray and bake for about 10 minutes in the pre-heated oven.

THE VERY BEST SHORTBREAD

MAKES 8 SHAPES OR WEDGES

INGREDIENTS

100 g (4 oz) plain flour
50 g (2 oz) semolina
100 g (4 oz) butter
50 g (2 oz) caster sugar

TO DECORATE
25 g (1 oz) flaked almonds
(optional)
caster or demerara sugar
for dusting

YOU WILL NEED

flat baking tray or 18 cm
(7 in) sandwich tin
mixing bowl or food
processor
palette knife
wire rack

GLACÉ CHERRIES, *dried apricots and sultanas could make a delicious and festive addition to this shortbread, which is traditionally eaten at Christmas and New Year, but the biscuits will then need to be eaten on the day of making, as they soon become soggy with the moisture from the fruit.*

PRE-HEAT THE OVEN TO 325°F/160°C/GAS 3. LIGHTLY GREASE A FLAT BAKING TRAY OR SANDWICH TIN.

Mix the flour with the semolina in a bowl or food processor. Add the butter and sugar and rub together with the fingertips, or process, until the mixture forms a smooth dough.

Place the dough on to the prepared baking tray and roll out to an 18 cm (7 in) circle. Crimp the edges to decorate and prick all over with a fork. Mark into 8 wedges, sprinkle with the flaked almonds if using, and chill until firm.

Bake in the oven for about 35 minutes or until a very pale golden brown. Re-mark the sections, dust with the caster sugar and leave to cool on the baking tray for about 5 minutes. Carefully lift off with a palette knife and cool on a wire rack.

Alternatively, press the dough out into a greased sandwich tin, bake as before and then mark into 8 wedges. (It will probably take slightly more time to bake in a sandwich tin.) Leave to cool in the tin and sprinkle with the sugar to decorate.

THE VERY BEST CHOCOLATE CAKE

MAKES 1 20 CM (8 IN) ROUND CAKE

INGREDIENTS

FOR THE CAKE MIXTURE
50 g (2 oz) cocoa
6 tablespoons boiling water
3 large eggs
120 ml (4 fl oz) milk
175 g (6 oz) self-raising flour
1 rounded teaspoon baking powder
100 g (4 oz) soft baking margarine
275 g (10 oz) caster sugar

FOR THE ICING AND FILLING
120 g (4½ oz) good chocolate, broken into small pieces
150 ml (5 fl oz) double cream
3 tablespoons apricot jam, slightly warmed

YOU WILL NEED

2 20 cm (8 in) sandwich tins
silicone paper or baking parchment
food processor
2 mixing bowls
wire rack
pan
small palette knife

IF YOU CAN'T *indulge in chocolate cake at this time of year, when can you? This is made in the food processor but it could be made in a conventional electric mixer without any problems.*

PRE-HEAT THE OVEN TO 350°F/180°C/GAS 4. GREASE AND BASE-LINE THE SANDWICH TINS AND SET ASIDE.

First process the cocoa and boiling water until well mixed. Add the remaining ingredients to the food processor and whiz for 1-2 minutes, scraping down the inside of the bowl if necessary. The mixture will be a thickish batter. Divide the mixture between the two prepared tins and then bake in the pre-heated oven for about 20 minutes until well risen and shrinking away from the sides of the tin. Carefully turn the cakes out and leave on a wire rack to cool.

Meanwhile, make the icing and filling by measuring the chocolate and cream together in a bowl. Stand the bowl in a pan of simmering water for about 10-15 minutes, stirring from time to time until the chocolate has melted. Then remove the bowl from the heat and leave it to become cold and almost set.

When the two sponges are completely cool, spread the tops of each of them with the apricot jam. Spread half the icing on top of one of the cakes and place the other cake on top of it before spreading over the remainder of the icing as a topping. Take the palette knife and, from the centre of the cake, draw large 's' shapes to give a swirl effect.

CHRISTMAS DAY COOKING

There is probably no other time quite like 25 December for such a concentrated cooking effort in almost every home. While it can be a frantic morning's worth of hard work, I find that a fair amount of planning beforehand, alongside the delegation of the table laying and washing up, makes my own life easier. The team of us who work on the programme have compiled our own Christmas Week Countdown (see page 126) to help you remember everything. But here I offer you my own recipes for Christmas Day, which I have found have worked for me over the years when it has been my turn to be host.

ROAST TURKEY WITH SAUSAGEMEAT STUFFING

SERVES 10

INGREDIENTS

FOR THE ROASTING
5.5-6.5 kg (12-14 lb) free-range turkey
1 lemon, skin left on and wiped clean
1 onion, skinned
100 g (4 oz) butter

FOR THE STUFFING
900 g (2 lb) sausagemeat
turkey liver (taken from the giblets), chopped

(Cont. opposite)

I MUST SAY THAT *I do prefer to pay a little extra for a free-range bird, as you really can taste the difference. In my experience, an oven-ready turkey of about 5.5-6.5 kg (12-14 lb) should be enough to feed about 10 people. Make sure that your butcher or supplier gives you the giblets as these are a vital ingredient for the gravy (see Giblet Stock Gravy, page 25) and the stuffing!*

As soon as you get the turkey home, remove the giblets, wipe the bird clean, pat it dry and refrigerate it until you are ready to stuff it.

The stuffing can be made late on Christmas Eve. Mix together all the stuffing ingredients, making

2 packets of good quality sage-and-onion stuffing mix
900 ml (1½ pints) boiling water

___

YOU WILL NEED

mixing bowl
skewer
large roasting tin
loaf tin

sure that everything is well distributed. Place the lemon and onion in the cavity of the turkey. Then begin to stuff the bird. Work from the neck end, loosening the skin and gently pushing the stuffing mixture into place. When you are happy with the amount of stuffing, secure the flap of neck skin by threading a skewer through it. Place any remaining stuffing mixture in a loaf tin.

On Christmas Day, once you have worked out when you want to sit everyone down to eat, preheat the oven to 350°F/180°C/gas 4. Just before you are due to begin the cooking process, place the bird in the roasting tin and smear the skin of the turkey with half of the butter. Meanwhile, melt the remaining butter and soak the muslin square in it. This may sound odd but, ever since I was given this tip, I have considered it a stroke of genius. When you are satisfied that the muslin has absorbed all of the butter, drape it over the bird. As you will probably have guessed, the muslin remains over the turkey as it cooks and prevents it, especially the legs, from drying out.

A bird of this size should take about 4 hours in a slow oven (see chart on page 66). I cook with an Aga and place the roasting tin on the bottom set of runners. The beauty of the muslin square is that, despite the higher temperature, it will still ensure a moist bird.

To test that the turkey is properly cooked, insert a skewer into the deepest part of one of the thighs: the juices should run clear. When you are satisfied, remove the bird to 'rest' (preferably on its serving plate) in a warm place for half an hour. During this time you should cook the bacon rolls and chipolatas and make the gravy in the roasting tin.

WILD RICE AND SULTANA STUFFING

SERVES 10

INGREDIENTS

3 medium-sized onions,
finely chopped
175 g (6 oz) walnuts,
finely chopped
3 tablespoons parsley,
finely chopped
6 tablespoons sultanas
175 g (6 oz) wild rice,
6 tablespoons wholemeal
breadcrumbs
3 large eggs, beaten
salt and freshly ground
black pepper

YOU WILL NEED

mixing bowl
large loaf tin

THIS IS AN EXOTIC *alternative to the sausagemeat stuffing recipe on page 22. Soak the wild rice according to the instructions on the packet before you start.*

Combine all the ingredients in the mixing bowl and season to taste. Now stuff the bird according to the directions given for the Sausagemeat Stuffing on page 22, and place any remaining stuffing in the loaf tin. Check the loaf tin after about 25 minutes to make sure that it isn't cooking too quickly and drying out. (This stuffing takes a lot less time to cook than sausagemeat stuffing.)

Delia & Simon's Phone-in Top Tips

Every Christmas on the programme we are lucky enough to have the next best thing to having Delia Smith herself hovering at your elbow by the stove as you prepare your Christmas food. I am, of course, referring to our extremely popular phone-in, when listeners get the chance to quiz Delia and her good friend Simon Hopkinson, from the Bibendum restaurant in London and a regular contributor to *Sainsbury's The Magazine*. People ring asking for suggestions and help. The advice they receive is expert and inspirational so we've included the Top Tips from last year's phone-in in distinctive boxes throughout the book.

GIBLET STOCK GRAVY

INGREDIENTS

FOR THE STOCK
1 onion, chopped finely
2 sticks of celery, chopped finely
2 large carrots, chopped finely
50 g (2 oz) butter
turkey giblets (except for the liver, which you will be using in the stuffing)
1.2 litres (2 pints) water
bunch of fresh thyme or 1 teaspoon of dried thyme

FOR THE GRAVY
2 tablespoons plain flour

YOU WILL NEED

pan
sieve
covered bowl to store

THIS IS SOMETHING *you can begin to make a little ahead of the Christmas Day rush.*

One or two days before Christmas, depending on when you collect your turkey, brown the onion, celery and carrot in the butter. Meanwhile, rinse the giblets and then add these to the pan along with the thyme. Cover the pan and leave the stock to simmer gently for a couple of hours. Remove the pan from the heat and strain the stock through a sieve into the container in which you will be storing it until Christmas Day.

On the day, once the turkey is properly roasted and has been removed from the roasting tin, add the flour to the meat juices and stir, over a moderate heat, until the flour has absorbed all the delicious meat juices and the gravy begins to bubble a little. Now add a little of the giblet stock and continue stirring, making sure that any lumps of flour are dispersed. Continue to stir as you add as much of the stock as you require. The flour will thicken the gravy, and it can be served as soon as it is piping hot and has reached its best pouring consistency.

BACON ROLLS AND CHIPOLATA SAUSAGES

INGREDIENTS

vegetable oil
rashers of smoked bacon,
  de-rinded (allow at least
  2 bacon rolls per person)
chipolatas (again, allow at
  least two per guest)

YOU WILL NEED

small roasting tin
pastry brush
cocktail sticks

I FIND THAT THESE *simple foods are extremely popular with children (of all ages!) at Christmas lunch. If you are lucky enough to have a cool larder, you could prepare the bacon rolls late on Christmas Eve. Otherwise, make them up first thing in the morning and put them safely out of the way until it's nearly lunch time.*

Lightly brush the base of the roasting tin with the vegetable oil and then keep the tin close to hand. Take the first rasher of bacon and roll this up very tightly before skewering it into position with a cocktail stick. Do the same with the other rashers of bacon, placing each one in the roasting tin in neat lines as you go. Now line up the chipolatas alongside the bacon rolls.

Place the roasting tin in the oven as soon as you have removed the turkey for its 'rest'. Turn the bacon rolls and chipolatas over after about 5-10 minutes. They should be cooked, depending on how well your oven is coping with all that intense cooking, in about another 5-10 minutes. Ideally, the bacon rolls should be really crisp but you don't want the chipolatas 'tough', so do keep an eye on them and remove them before the bacon if necessary. Place the rolls and the chipolatas around the 'resting' turkey on its serving plate so that they keep warm until ready to serve.

BACON AND WATER CHESTNUT ROLLS

INGREDIENTS

vegetable oil
1 large tin of Chinese
water chestnuts, very
well rinsed
rashers of smoked bacon,
de-rinded (allow 1-2
rashers per person)

YOU WILL NEED

small roasting tin
pastry brush
cocktail sticks

I WAS GIVEN THIS recipe by a friend, and it is a varia-tion on the traditional bacon rolls. The crispness of the bacon contrasts well with the crunchiness of the water chestnuts. Do be sure, though, to rinse the chestnuts with water thoroughly so that they lose the 'tinny' taste they can otherwise have.

Lightly brush the base of the roasting tin with the vegetable oil. Make sure that the water chestnuts aren't too wet (pat them dry with some kitchen paper if necessary) before you simply wrap them tightly with the rashers of bacon, one chestnut per rasher, and spear each one into position with a cocktail stick. Cook them exactly as you do the traditional Bacon Rolls (see page 26). To add vari-ation, I sometimes make up a mixture of the two types of rolls to serve with the turkey.

You will probably have some of the water chestnuts left over. I usually put these in a covered container in the fridge and use them in a turkey stir-fry a day or so later.

ROASTED POTATOES

INGREDIENTS

*potatoes - allow about
100 g (4 oz) for the
average adult's appetite
boiling water, salted
vegetable oil*

YOU WILL NEED

*large pan with lid
strainer
roasting tin
serving bowl, warmed to
very hot*

WHO CAN BEAT *good old plain roast potatoes? Just in case this is your 'first' Christmas, here is the way I do them. I think they taste best if cooked around the turkey itself, but if you don't have a large enough tin, roast them separately. Start cooking them about 1½ hours before you want to eat.*

First peel the potatoes and cut them into even-sized pieces (I usually cut each medium-sized potato into four). Rinse the potatoes and then place them in a pan of boiling water to simmer for about 8-10 minutes, depending on the number of potatoes you are cooking. Drain the potatoes, pop them back into the saucepan, put the lid on and give the pan a few serious shakes.

If you are roasting your potatoes around the turkey, remove the roasting tin from the oven, remembering to shut the oven door to keep the heat in. Now distribute the potatoes evenly around your already roasting turkey, making sure that each potato is generously coated with the juices which will, by now, have oozed from the bird. Add more vegetable oil to coat the potatoes if necessary. Return the roasting tin to the oven as soon as possible to avoid dropping the bird's temperature too much. If you are roasting the potatoes in a separate roasting tin, make sure that it is piping hot before you add the potatoes: it's best to warm it in the roasting oven for at least 30 minutes before you start.

Your potatoes will probably need at least 60-70 minutes to roast properly and will need to be turned over half-way through their cooking time. (If you've got all your timings very well co-ordinated, your turkey should be roasted and ready to remove from the oven to 'rest' at the same time as you are turning your potatoes.) I always check my potatoes after about 45 minutes to make sure that they are cooking evenly – and to make sure that they aren't overcooking, which can sometimes be the case in my Aga! Generally though, I find that the oven is working overtime with the turkey and all its trimmings, so regular, but not interfering, checking is best.

As soon as your potatoes are roasted (they should be a deep golden brown with a fairly crisp outer coating, but soft inside), transfer them to the piping hot serving bowl. It's best to serve the potatoes as soon as possible but, if you are slightly ahead of yourself with them, keep them in a very warm place until you are ready to eat.

Delia & Simon's Phone-in Top Tips

Irene Elton from Essex was cooking for four and wanted to know what size of goose she should buy that would give generous portions.

Always get the biggest one possible, Delia advised, as there is very little meat on a goose. About 5-5.5 kg (11-12 lb) would be best. Any left-over meat would be delicious served in sandwiches the next day. Simon also thought the cold goose would taste good with bread sauce. A recipe for bread sauce is on page 34.

ROASTED PARSNIPS

INGREDIENTS

parsnips - allow about 100 g (4 oz) for the average adult's appetite boiling water, salted (if the parsnips are thick and chunky) vegetable oil

YOU WILL NEED

pan
strainer
small roasting tin
serving bowl, warmed to very hot

IT'S A FAMILY *joke that I always serve parsnips! This is the best method I've tried for roasting them successfully.*

After peeling and washing the parsnips, cut them into even-sized chunks. I blanch bigger pieces for about a minute in boiling water and then add them to a small roasting tin with a little vegetable oil (or around the turkey if there is enough room) in the oven. They should take about 35-45 minutes to cook.

If the parsnips are thin ones, I don't bother to blanch them and just toss them into the roasting tin with the potatoes about 20-25 minutes before the potatoes should be ready. When they are cooked I transfer them straight into the piping-hot serving bowl.

Delia & Simon's Phone-in Top Tips

Pauline in Gloucester asked for recipes for sweet potatoes, which she wanted to serve as an alternative with her turkey.

Cut the sweet potatoes into wedges and par-boil them first, said Delia. Then roast them, finishing off with a little butter and a sprinkling of cinnamon - just like the Americans do at Thanksgiving.

BRUSSELS SPROUTS
WITH FLAKED ALMONDS

INGREDIENTS

*Brussels sprouts - allow
about 100 g (4 oz) per
adult
flaked almonds - allow
about 25 g (1 oz) per
100 g (4 oz) of sprouts
boiling water, salted
about 50 g (2 oz) butter
vegetable oil
salt*

YOU WILL NEED

*large pan
strainer
frying pan
serving bowl, thoroughly
warmed*

I ALWAYS THINK *you have to be a little careful not to overload Christmas lunch with too many contrasting and competing flavours. Quite often I leave the vegetables fairly plain so that their own flavour comes to the fore. Having said that, I hope that you will enjoy this variation on a theme as much as my family did last Christmas.*

First, cut a cross on the bottom of each sprout so that they cook evenly. You can cook the almonds and the sprouts simultaneously. Start by boiling the salted water for the Brussels sprouts and add the vegetables as soon as the water comes to the boil. Depending on the amount of vegetables you are boiling, they should boil for about 8-10 minutes. You don't want to cook them for too long or they will become 'soggy' and their 'greeness' will dull. (Test to see if they are cooked by inserting a sharp knife or skewer into one of the sprouts: it should go in easily but the sprout should still be firm.)

Meanwhile, shallow-fry the almonds in the butter and a dash of vegetable oil (which prevents the butter burning), stirring frequently, until they are a golden colour. Be careful not to overdo the almonds, as they will burn relatively quickly. Remove the almonds from the butter and place them in the serving bowl ready for the Brussels sprouts to join them. (If necessary, keep the bowl in a hot place until the sprouts are cooked.)

BUTTERED CARROTS

INGREDIENTS

carrots, scrubbed clean –
allow about 100 g (4 oz)
for the average adult's
appetite
boiling water, salted
50-75 g (2-3 oz) butter

YOU WILL NEED

pan
strainer
serving bowl, warmed
to very hot

CARROTS ARE SUCH *a delicious vegetable that I prefer to cook them quite simply and serve them tossed in butter.*

Cut the carrots into even-sized pieces and place the carrot pieces into the saucepan of boiling, salted water. Simmer for about 8-10 minutes. When they are cooked, you should be able to insert a knife into them – but you don't want them to be soggy or they will lose their flavour. Drain the carrots and place them in the serving bowl. Top them with the butter and toss gently. Serve immediately, or keep them in a very warm place until lunch is ready to serve.

*Delia &
Simon's
Phone-in
Top Tips*

Carol from Twickenham asked for help with cooking wild boar, which she fancied as an alternative to the usual turkey.

The answer was simple: Delia suggested using her favourite pork recipes as the cooking was the same and the results delicious. For wild boar read pork – it's as simple as that.

PRUNES IN ARMAGNAC

SERVES 10

INGREDIENTS

450 g (1 lb) prunes with stones (prunes from Agen are the best)
900 ml (1½ pints) strong tea
100 g (4 oz) granulated sugar
120 ml (4 fl oz) water
300 ml (10 fl oz) Armagnac

YOU WILL NEED

pan
covered bowl
bowl

THIS IS A GREAT *accompaniment to any roast poultry dish - at any time of the year!*

Place the prunes in the pan and cover them with the tea. Simmer for 5 minutes and then remove them from the heat. Pour the prunes and the tea into the covered bowl and leave them to soak overnight.

The next day, dissolve the sugar in the water in the pan and bring it to the boil. Allow it to bubble for 2 minutes and then pour it in to a bowl. Drain the prunes, discarding the tea, and add the prunes to the sugar water along with the Armagnac. Keep them warm until ready to serve.

Delia & Simon's Phone-in Top Tips

Mrs Doreen Stafford of Shropshire wanted to know how to get a nice moist jelly into a game pie.

Delia advised Mrs Stafford to make up a jellied stock with the scraps of game left-over from her pie, adding some gelatine. A ratio of 1 sachet of gelatine per pint of stock is best - this can be scaled down according to the amount required. When the pie is cool, pour the jelly in (Simon suggested making a little funnel out of tin foil to do this easily) and it sets all around the ingredients.

BREAD SAUCE

SERVES 10

INGREDIENTS

900 ml (1½ pints milk
2 small onions, whole,
studded with 8-10 cloves
each
175 g (6 oz) white bread,
crusts removed
salt and freshly ground
black pepper to taste

YOU WILL NEED

pan with lid
whisk

M Y FAMILY'S *Christmas wouldn't be complete with-out this. Don't waste time making breadcrumbs, as the whole slices of bread will disintegrate during cooking.*

Place all the ingredients in the pan and set it over a low heat, half covered. Keep an eye on the pan and, as it heats, break up the bread with a wooden spoon. Once the sauce begins to boil, whisk it, preferably with a balloon whisk, or stir it vigorously until it is well mixed. Remove the bread sauce from the heat and set aside until you are ready to heat it gently to serve. If the sauce is too thick when re-heating, add a little more milk and stir it in.

Delia & Simon's Phone-in Top Tips

M rs Chris Pickthall from Merseyside phoned in to ask how she should defrost and roast her frozen 5 kg (11 lb) free-range goose. Delia advised Mrs Pick-thall to defrost the goose for about 24 hours in the refrigerator (on the lowest shelf) in order to defrost the bird slowly and help it to retain its juices. As for cooking, both Simon and Delia stressed that it was essential to prick the skin of the goose before roasting so that the fat could be released during the cooking time - in fact it's best to pour off the fat twice as it roasts. (Use the fat to make beautiful roast potatoes afterwards!) For stuffing ideas, Delia had a wonderful idea for mixing a basic sage and onion stuffing with pork sausage-meat and the chopped goose liver.

WHITE CHOCOLATE CHEESECAKE

MAKES 1 22 CM (8½ IN) ROUND CAKE

INGREDIENTS

FOR THE BASE
175 g (6 oz) unsalted butter
75 g (3 oz) caster sugar
75 g (3 oz) white chocolate, grated
350 g (12 oz) plain flour, sifted
3 egg yolks
75 g (3 oz) unsalted butter, melted

FOR THE TOPPING
300 ml (½ pint) whipping or double cream
3 large eggs, separated
75 g (3 oz) caster sugar
225 g (8 oz) full-fat soft cheese
225 g (8 oz) good-quality white chocolate, melted
20 g (¾ oz) gelatine powder
3 tablespoons brandy, warmed

YOU WILL NEED

2 mixing bowls
rolling pin
flat baking tray
22 cm (8½ in) flan tin, with removable base
small bowl

MY CHILDREN *tend to find a traditional Christmas Pudding a little rich for their taste and not all adults like it either. I first made this cheesecake as an alternative a couple of years ago, and it is now a favourite. You can make it look festive by adding a sprig of holly and some decorative silver balls (the type used as cake decorations).*

PRE-HEAT THE OVEN TO 350°F/180°C/GAS 4.

Make the base first by thoroughly blending the butter and sugar. Add the grated chocolate and flour and stir before adding the egg yolks and mixing well. Roll out the mixture into a rough rectangle shape. Bake this on the baking tray until quite firm - it should take about 10-15 minutes. Then remove it from the oven and set it aside to cool before breaking it up into crumbs (you could do this in a food processor). Place the crumbs into a clean bowl and add the melted butter. Stir well and then press the mixture into a flan dish, making sure that you line the sides as well as the base. Leave it aside to cool.

Whisk the cream until stiff. In a separate bowl, whisk the egg yolks and the sugar together until light and foamy. Add the full-fat soft cheese and the melted chocolate. Now, in a small bowl, dissolve the gelatine in the warmed brandy. When it is ready, add the melted gelatine to the soft cheese mixture and whisk until smooth before folding in the stiffened cream.

Lightly whisk the egg whites in a clean mixing bowl. When they are ready, fold these in to the creamy mixture and then pour everything into the crumbed base. Leave it in the refrigerator to set for 3-4 hours. Carefully remove the cheesecake from the tin and, if desired, serve it with vanilla ice-cream or more whipped cream.

BRANDY CREAM SAUCE

INGREDIENTS

3 small egg yolks
300 ml (10 fl oz) double cream, whipped
3 tablespoons golden syrup, warmed
2 tablespoons brandy

YOU WILL NEED

bowl
whisk

MARY BERRY'S *Brandy Cream (see page 17) is quite delicious but a friend gave me this recipe* which also goes brilliantly with Mary's scrumptious Byre Farm Christmas Pudding (page 16).

In the bowl, whisk the egg yolks until creamy. Fold in the cream and then add the golden syrup and brandy. You can make this on Christmas Eve and keep it covered in the fridge or you can freeze it to make ice-cream.

 LISTENER'S TIP

NOT SO MUCH *a recipe as a tip, this time from Jane Edmond in Buckinghamshire who dislikes candied peel in cakes, puddings and particularly mince-meat and has created this alternative.*

Use chopped no-soak apricots or chopped traditional dried apricots soaked in brandy first. Simply add them to recipes in place of the required quantity of candied peel - delicious.

NADINE ABENSUR'S VEGETARIAN CHRISTMAS LUNCH SUGGESTIONS

Nadine Abensur, the Food Director of Cranks vegetarian restaurants, is always a popular guest on the programme. I immediately thought of enlisting Nadine's help to find delicious recipes for vegetarian guests at the Christmas lunch table. These dishes will look stunning and excite the tastebuds of all your family and friends - vegetarian or not.

GOATS' CHEESE WITH FIG AND ONION CONFIT

SERVES 6

INGREDIENTS

FOR THE CONFIT
450 g (1 lb) baby onions
85 ml (3 fl oz) sunflower oil
1 garlic clove, crushed
1 small piece of root
  ginger, grated
1 tablespoon brandy
juice of ½ orange
zest of 1 orange
250 ml (8 fl oz) water or
  vegetable stock
salt and freshly ground
  black pepper
450 g (1 lb) soft dried figs,
  chopped into slivers
(Cont. overleaf)

THE SWEET, *sharp, tangy confit cuts through the richness of the goats' cheese and creates a starter with enough glamour for a special occasion that still allows space for the party fare to follow.*

Blanch the baby onions for 1 minute to loosen the skins, then peel. Heat the oil in a pan and then add the onions, garlic and ginger along with the brandy, orange juice and zest, and the vegetable stock. Bring the mixture to the boil and then allow it to simmer for at least 10 minutes, until the liquid is reduced to less than half. Season with salt and pepper and then add the figs and continue to simmer until the juices are well reduced to a thick coating consistency.

TO SERVE
*mixed leaves, including
frisée, rocket, lambs'
lettuce, and radicchio
olive oil
salt and freshly ground
black pepper
6 individual goats' cheeses
toasted walnut bread*

To serve, toss the mixed leaves in a bowl with olive oil, salt and pepper. Place a mound of leaves on each serving plate, then top them with a goats' cheese. Spoon the confit on top and serve at once with rounds of toasted walnut bread.

YOU WILL NEED

*pan
mixing bowl
6 serving plates*

Delia & Simon's Phone-in Top Tips

Jonathan Edens from Cornwall was helping his mother cater for his sister and she would be the only vegetarian at the table. Could Delia and Simon offer any bright ideas for vegetarian alternatives to turkey for one person?

Simon was quick to respond with a recipe for a warm lentil salad made with French Puy lentils. Cook them in water (follow the instructions on the packet of lentils) with very finely chopped up vegetables, carrots, celery, onion and leeks. Don't add the salt until the end of the cooking or it will make the lentils go hard. When everything is tender, drain and mix in a little Dijon mustard, a touch of vinegar and some olive oil. Serve still warm, dressed with some finely chopped spring onions or chives, and a touch of garlic. Add a couple of poached eggs to the top of the salad.

Delia had another idea. Make up some choux pastry with a little cheese in it, shape it into a little puff and bake it in a hot oven, then fill it with mushrooms that you have cooked slowly in Madeira. If you can get some, add some dried porcini to the mushrooms. Warm through just before you are ready to serve lunch.

WILD MUSHROOM FRICASSÉE

SERVES 6

INGREDIENTS

150 g (5 oz) dried assorted
wild mushrooms
600 ml (1 pint) hot water
1 tablespoon tamari
1 tablespoon brandy
2 garlic cloves, crushed
½ teaspoon grain mustard
40 g (1½ oz) butter
¼ teaspoon soft brown
sugar
2 large sprigs of fresh
tarragon
100 g (4 oz) shiitake
mushrooms, tough ends
removed
150 g (5 oz) oyster
mushrooms
150 g (5 oz) chanterelles,
carefully cleaned
2 spring onions, finely
sliced
175 g (6 oz) baby spinach
1 tablespoon double cream
salt and freshly ground
black pepper

YOU WILL NEED

2 mixing bowls
muslin
frying pan

FOR A FESTIVE presentation, serve this on slices of toasted brioche or use it as a filling for a traditional-looking puff pastry Wellington. If you prefer a more modern approach serve with soft polenta.

First soak the dried mushrooms in the hot water together with the tamari and brandy until they have 'puffed up'. Strain them through muslin into another bowl to remove any gritty bits and then return them to the liquid. Place them in the frying pan with the water and bring them to the boil with the crushed garlic, mustard and butter, stirring continuously.

Now add the sugar and the whole sprigs of tarragon. Continue to stir occasionally as the juices reduce to about half their original volume. Add the shiitake mushrooms and carefully stir these in for just a minute. Then add the chanterelles carefully before removing the wilted sprigs of tarragon. After about a minute, add the spring onions and spinach until it just wilts. Remove the pan from the heat and stir in the cream and season to taste. Serve the fricassée at once.

PARMESAN AND CHIVE THINS WITH AVOCADO MOUSSE

SERVES 6

INGREDIENTS

FOR THE PARMESAN THINS
450 g (1 lb) plain white
    flour
1 teaspoon salt
275 g (10 oz) unsalted
    butter, cut into small
    cubes
25 g (1 oz) freshly grated
    Parmesan
1 garlic clove, crushed
juice and zest of 1 lemon
3-4 whole chives, finely
    chopped
3 tablespoons very cold
    water

FOR THE AVOCADO MOUSSE
2 ripe Hass avocados
4 tablespoons water
2 tablespoons light olive oil
salt and freshly ground
    black pepper
1 garlic clove, finely
    crushed
1 long basil leaf, finely
    shredded
2 spring onions, finely
    chopped
1 corn cob, blanched, with
    the kernels scraped off

(Cont. opposite)

THE PASTRY *must be as light and crisp as possible to contrast with the softness of the mousse. Make the mousse at the last minute to prevent the avocado from oxidizing and turning brown.*

First make the pastry for the Parmesan thins. Sift the flour into a mixing bowl together with the salt. Add the butter cubes to the flour and rub together lightly with your fingers until the mixture resembles breadcrumbs. Now add the Parmesan, the garlic, lemon zest, chives, and finally the water and lemon juice to bring the dough together. Wrap the dough in cling film and refrigerate for 30 minutes. Meanwhile, pre-heat the oven to 400°F/200°C/gas 6.

When the pastry is cold enough, roll it out on a well-floured surface as thinly as possible. You can then either cut the pastry with a pastry cutter or tear the pastry gently into rough, 10 cm (4 in) circular shapes. You need 18 circles, but make a few extra as they are so fragile that you might break a couple of them. Place the pastry circles onto the baking tray and bake them for about 10 minutes or until crisp and beginning to bubble. Remove them from the baking tray immediately and place them on a cooling rack.

To make the mousse, peel the avocados and place the flesh in a blender with the water, oil, salt and pepper, and garlic. Blend until the mixture is smooth

FOR THE GARNISH
2 tomatoes, deseeded and
  finely chopped
handful of small basil
  leaves
85 ml (3 fl oz) olive oil
1 teaspoon balsamic
  vinegar

YOU WILL NEED

mixing bowl
cling film
rolling pin
10 cm (4 in) round pastry
  cutter (optional)
baking tray, lightly floured
cooling rack
blender or food processor
6 serving plates

and light and gently fold in the basil, spring onion, and the blanched corn kernels.

To assemble the Parmesan thins, place one pastry circle onto a serving plate and then lightly add a tablespoon of the mousse. Place another pastry circle on the top, then more mousse, and then, finally, a third pastry circle. (Work carefully to avoid breakage.) Garnish the Parmesan thins with the tomatoes, fresh basil, and olive oil flavoured with the balsamic vinegar. Serve at once.

Delia &
Simon's
Phone-in
Top Tips

Keith called from Ross-on-Wye wanting to know how to keep the tops on his flaky pastry mince pies as they baked.

Clamp them down, Delia and Simon cried in unison! The problem with any kind of pie, said Delia, was the temptation to stretch the pastry across the top. It was best, she advised, to make the lids a little bigger than the top of the pie so that you are actually squeezing it together rather than stretching over the top. Dampen the edges together with an egg wash or just milk and then, taking a pair of scissors, make three little snips on the top of each pie to let the steam out. As Simon said, the steam has to get out somewhere and if it can't get out, it'll push the pastry up.

MUSHROOM STRUDEL

SERVES 6-8

INGREDIENTS

100 ml (3½ fl oz) sunflower oil
250 g (9 oz) onions, diced
750 g (1½ lb) leeks, chopped finely
1 large garlic clove, crushed
1.5 kg (3¼ lb) mushrooms, whole
85 ml (3 fl oz) tamari or soy sauce
handful of fresh tarragon, or mixed tarragon and basil
25 g (1 oz) carrots, grated
50 g (2 oz) dried cranberries, soaked in
60 ml (2¼ fl oz) brandy
400 g (14 oz) couscous
750 g (1½ lb) puff pastry (there will be some left over)
flour for rolling out
1 small egg, beaten
salt and freshly ground black pepper

YOU WILL NEED

pan with lid
baking tray, lightly greased and floured

THIS IS A GREAT recipe to use at Christmas as you can make it and freeze ahead.

PRE-HEAT THE OVEN TO 425°F/220°C/GAS 7.

In a pan, heat the oil and fry the onion until golden brown and tender. Add the leeks and continue to sauté, stirring frequently, until they are tender. Season with salt and pepper and the garlic. Now add the mushrooms and, when they seem nearly cooked, add the tamari or soy sauce along with the herbs, carrots and the cranberries with the brandy. Cook for a few minutes, stirring all the time. Remove from the heat before adding the couscous, stirring while it absorbs the liquid. Cover the pan and set aside to cool.

On a lightly floured surface, roll out the puff pastry into two 35 x 30 cm (14 x 12 in) rectangles, no thicker than 3 mm (⅛ in). Place the cooked mixture in a long sausage-like shape down the middle of each of the two pastry pieces - about 9 cm (3½ in) wide and high, leaving a gap at either end. Bring the pastry up so that it meets in the middle and pinch it firmly all the way along, tucking in the ends neatly. Carefully transfer each of the strudels onto the baking tray and then brush them generously with the beaten egg. With the point of a knife, make small diagonal cuts on both sides of the join. Place the baking sheet in the oven and bake for about 25 minutes or until a rich golden colour. Either serve the strudel at once, or cool and refrigerate or freeze.

COUSCOUS ROYALE

SERVES 6

INGREDIENTS

about 600 ml (1 pint)
vegetable stock
6 medium-sized carrots
1 kg (2¼ lb) pumpkin,
unpeeled and cut into
7.5 cm (3 in) pieces
½ small white cabbage,
cut into 5 cm (2 in)
chunks
450 g (1 lb) dried chick
peas, soaked overnight
1 onion, peeled but left
whole
1 bay leaf
1 stick celery
1 garlic clove
12 baby onions, peeled
2 tablespoons caster sugar
150 ml (5 fl oz) sunflower
oil
6 medium-sized leeks, cut
into 5 cm (2 in) pieces
6 medium-sized
courgettes, cut into larger
chunks
a few strands saffron,
soaked in 50 ml (2 fl oz)
very hot water
75 g (3 oz) sultanas, soaked
in a hot vegetable stock
for 10 minutes

(Cont. overleaf)

THIS IS AN impressive dish to look at - and it tastes as good as it looks.

Half fill the pan with vegetable stock. Cut 5 of the carrots into large chunks and add these to the stock with the pumpkin and cabbage. Bring everything to the boil and simmer for 5-10 minutes. Strain the vegetables, reserving the stock, and set aside.

Place the chick peas with the onion and the remaining whole carrot, the bay leaf, celery and garlic into a large pan with 750 ml (1¼ pints) of water and simmer for 1½ hours.

Whilst you are waiting for the chick peas to cook, pre-heat the oven to 350°F/180°F/gas 4.

Now cook the vegetables, adding salt and pepper to taste as each is cooked. Place the baby onions in a heavy-based pan with 250 ml (8 fl oz) water, sprinkle with about half of the sugar and a little salt and pepper. Sauté until golden brown and tender and the water has evaporated. Set aside. Heat 1 tablespoon of the oil in a frying pan and sauté the leeks until they are lightly browned. Remove from the pan and set aside. In the same frying pan, sauté the courgettes until lightly browned.

Now place half of the leeks, half of the courgettes and all of the cabbage in an ovenproof dish with 120 ml (4 fl oz) of the reserved vegetable stock. Add 1 tablespoon of the oil to the dish, along with

6 medium-sized parsnips, cut into chunks
½ teaspoon ground cinnamon
450 g (1 lb) couscous
a few strands saffron
175 g (6 oz) dried chestnuts, soaked overnight
1 handful of coriander and parsley, chopped finely
15 g (½ oz) butter
salt and freshly ground black pepper

YOU WILL NEED

pan
large pan
heavy-based pan
frying pan
2 ovenproof dishes with lids
large, round serving plate

1 teaspoon of the saffron stock and salt and pepper to taste. Cover the dish and bake it in the pre-heated oven for 25 minutes until tender and lightly browned. Now place the pumpkin, carrots, chick peas, baby onions, sultanas, parsnips, the rest of the leeks and courgettes and the chestnuts in a second ovenproof dish. Sprinkle with the rest of the sugar and the cinnamon, cover and bake for 25 minutes.

For the couscous, first heat the remaining vegetable stock until boiling and dissolve the remaining strands of saffron in this. Now place the couscous in a bowl and pour over sufficient boiling stock and stir until it swells and there is no trace of grittiness left in it. Add the coriander and parsley with the butter, mixing gently.

Serve the couscous at once: place it in a high mound on the plate and moisten it with a little more of the stock if necessary.

LISTENER'S RECIPE

CARDINAL MULLED WINE

INGREDIENTS

600 ml (1 pint) hot water
100 g (4 oz) barley sugar
3 cinnamon sticks
nutmeg, mace, and cardamom, to taste, or a packet of spices for mulled wine
2 tangerines
1 litre (1¼ pints) Spanish red wine

I'M GRATEFUL TO *Susan Wray of Hertfordshire who kindly sent me this recipe which she has been making for the past 25 years.*

Pour the water into a large pan and add the barley sugar, stirring gently until it melts. Now add the spices and the tangerines and simmer gently for about 15 minutes. Just before you are ready to serve, pour the wine into the saucepan and keep the mulled wine just warm. Never allow it to boil or it will impair the flavour.

KEVIN WOODFORD'S FESTIVE SUPPER-PARTY RECIPES

We are delighted when Kevin Woodford, well known for his flying television appearances, finds time to come on to the programme. Last year he generously allowed us to auction a gourmet weekend, spent mostly at his Isle of Man restaurants, for Children in Need. Here Kevin shares with us some of his favourite special supper-party recipes. Each dish is scrumptious and could be a star turn with other courses that are not so rich.

CARAMELIZED TARTLETS OF PEAR AND LEEK

SERVES 4

INGREDIENTS

75 g (3 oz) plain white flour
40 g (1½ oz) wholemeal flour
65 g (2½ oz) margarine
20 g (¾ oz) clear honey
50 g (2 oz) baby leeks, chopped finely
zest and juice of ½ an orange
2 firm pears
2 large eggs
150 ml (5 fl oz) double cream
15 g (½ oz) caster sugar

(Cont. overleaf)

THIS UNUSUAL *combination of ingredients yields a delicious surprise. The leeks take on a sweetness from the orange juice and will have your supper guests guessing as to what they are.*

PRE-HEAT THE OVEN TO 375°F/190°C/GAS 5.

Sift the plain flour into the mixing bowl and then add the wholemeal flour. Add the margarine and rub it in until the mixture resembles breadcrumbs. Add the honey and mix everything together to form a dough. On a lightly floured surface, roll out the dough and use it to line the moulds. Prick the pastry with a fork and bake the pastry cases blind in the pre-heated oven for 12-15 minutes until golden brown. Leave them to cool in the moulds. Don't turn off the oven!

65 g (2½ oz) demerara sugar
freshly ground black pepper

TO GARNISH
fresh pear slices

YOU WILL NEED

2 mixing bowls
sieve
rolling pin
4 individual Yorkshire pudding moulds
pan
whisk

Meanwhile, put the leeks, orange zest and juice in a pan and cook for 5 minutes until tender. Leave the pan to one side to cool. Then core, peel and thinly slice the pears and put them to one side. In a mixing bowl, whisk together the eggs, cream, both of the sugars and then pour these into a jug.

Fill the pastry cases with the leeks and season lightly with pepper. Arrange the pear slices on top and then pour over the cream mixture. Bake the tartlets in the oven for about 15 minutes until the custard has set. You could serve the tartlets garnished with more slices of uncooked pear.

Delia & Simon's Phone-in Top Tips

Jean Rollinson rang from Surrey, anxious to maintain an *entente cordiale*: her son's French girlfriend was bringing over her family (all seven of them!) for Christmas, and Jean wanted to prepare a British gastronomic spread.

Of course, Delia and Simon were brimming with ideas. A traditional roast turkey with all the trimmings was a must for Christmas Day - followed by Christmas pudding. For Christmas Eve, they suggested a ham served with Cumberland sauce, which is made by melting redcurrant jelly with Port and then adding grated orange and lemon zest with a little bit of English mustard powder (French mustard would make it go cloudy and, anyway, it's French!) and ground ginger. For Boxing Day, prior to a selection of cold cuts of turkey and ham, they suggested a starter of really good Scottish smoked salmon accompanied by scrambled egg. And Simon had a good tip for preparing the eggs for so many people: make them ahead by cooking them very slowly and adding the cream at the end. They can then be served cold, as they will still be soft, on top of some baked croutons, and sprinkled with chives.

STUFFED LOIN OF PORK ON A BED OF LENTILS WITH CARAMELIZED APPLES

INGREDIENTS

4 boneless loin of pork
chops, about 100 g (4 oz)
each
100 g (4 oz) lean raw ham
1 medium egg yolk
120 ml (4 fl oz) double
cream
pinch of cayenne pepper
1 tablespoon snipped fresh
chives
½ tablespoon vegetable oil
50 g (2 oz) smoked
streaky bacon, diced and
rind removed
50 g (2 oz) carrot, chopped
1 medium-sized onion,
chopped
50 g (2 oz) celery, chopped
75 g (3 oz) brown Puy
lentils, washed and
drained
450 ml (15 fl oz) chicken
stock
1 tablespoon chopped
fresh oregano
50 g (2 oz) butter
120 ml (4 fl oz) dry cider
75 g (3 oz) chilled butter,
cut into small pieces
2 large eating apples
75 g (3 oz) demerara
sugar
salt and black pepper
8 chervil leaves, to garnish

THIS RECIPE *produces a really delicious, moist dish and transforms a relatively plain, albeit tasty, joint of meat into a much more interesting one.*

PRE-HEAT THE OVEN TO 350°F/180°C/GAS 4.

Slice the pork chops lengthways, almost to the bottom, and open out. Place each piece between sheets of greaseproof paper and, using the rolling pin, beat until flattened. Mince the raw ham in a food processor, add the egg yolk and blend for 1 minute. Add the cream and mix until slightly thick. Season with cayenne, salt and pepper and mix in the chives. Chill for at least 30 minutes.

Heat the oil in a heavy-based flameproof casserole. Add the bacon and cook for 4 minutes. Add the vegetables and cook for a further 5 minutes, stirring frequently. Add the lentils, most of the stock, oregano and season with salt and pepper. Bring to the boil, then cover. Cook for 40-45 minutes until tender, stirring occasionally and adding more stock during cooking if necessary so that the mixture does not dry out. Check and, if necessary, adjust the seasoning.

Spread the chilled ham mixture evenly over the pork steaks. Roll them up like swiss rolls and secure with either string or cocktail sticks. Heat the butter in an ovenproof casserole, add the pork rolls and cook until sealed and just lightly browned. Add the cider and cover. Cook in the oven for 30-40 minutes until

YOU WILL NEED

greaseproof paper
rolling pin
food processor
2 heavy-based ovenproof
  casseroles with lids
string or cocktail sticks
baking tray
4 dariole moulds or ramekin
  dishes

tender. Remove the pork rolls from the liquid and keep warm. Place the casserole on a high heat, bring to the boil and reduce to one-third. Remove from the heat and gently shake the pan while adding the chilled pieces of butter. Do not reheat the sauce. Core and cut the apples into thick slices. Cover the apple slices with the sugar. Place on a buttered baking tray and caramelize either under the grill or in the oven. Put the lentil mixture into the moulds and turn out onto large plates. Remove the string from the pork, slice each piece of meat into 4 thick rounds and place these around the lentil puddings. Place the apples to the side of the meat and surround with the sauce. Garnish with the chervil and serve.

LISTENER'S RECIPE

APPLE MINCEMEAT

INGREDIENTS

225 g (8 oz) soft brown
sugar
200 ml (7 fl oz) apple
juice
1 kg (2¼ lb) cooking
apples, peeled, cored
and chopped
1 teaspoon mixed spice
225 g (8 oz) currants
225 g (8 oz) raisins
120 g (4½ oz) glacé
cherries, finely chopped
zest and juice of 1 lemon
85 ml (3 fl oz) brandy

B ELINDA DUNSTAN-CRAREY *from Ilkley kindly sent me her family's Apple Mincemeat recipe.*

Place the sugar and apple juice into a preserving pan and heat over a low heat until the sugar has dissolved. Add the apples and stir. Now add the rest of the ingredients, except the brandy, and bring slowly to the boil, stirring continuously. Lower the heat, half-cover the pan and simmer for about 30 minutes until reduced to a soft pulp. Remove from the heat and allow to cool before stirring in the brandy. Place the mincemeat in sterile jars and cover with a waxed circle to seal the top before closing the jar with a screw-top lid.

BITTER CHOCOLATE TART

SERVES 4-6

INGREDIENTS

175 g (6 oz) plain flour
25 g (1 oz) icing sugar
75 g (3 oz) unsalted butter
3 large egg yolks
1 tablespoon cold water
1 large egg
250 ml (8 fl oz) double cream
150 ml (5 fl oz) milk
450 g (1 lb) best-quality bitter couverture chocolate

YOU WILL NEED

2 mixing bowls
cling film
rolling pin
20 cm (8 in) flan tin with a removable base
foil
whisk
2 pans
small bowl

THE BITTERSWEET taste of this tart is the perfect ending for a supper party. There should be enough to feed 4-6, so you might just have enough left to offer the smallest of second helpings. Serve it warm or cold, with single cream.

Sift the flour and sugar together in a bowl. Add the butter and rub in to form a sandy mixture. Form a well in the centre of the mixture and add one of the egg yolks and the water. Mix everything together gently to form a dough. Wrap it in cling film and then chill in the refrigerator for 1 hour. Meanwhile pre-heat the oven to 400°F/200°C/gas 6.

Now roll out the pastry on a lightly floured surface and line the flan tin. Prick the base with a fork, line it with the foil and bake the pastry case blind for 10-15 minutes. Remove it from the oven and allow it to cool with the foil still in position. Reduce the oven temperature to 225°F/110°C/gas ¼ ready for baking the filled tart.

Whilst the case is baking, in a mixing bowl whisk together the whole egg and the two remaining egg yolks until light and fluffy. Set aside. Then combine the cream and milk in a pan and bring them to the boil. Remove this from the heat immediately and set aside to cool. Break the chocolate into pieces, place them in the small bowl and place the bowl over a pan of boiling water. Allow the chocolate to melt and then remove it from the heat. Let the chocolate cool but not so much that it resets. Now combine the egg mixture with the cream and milk and the chocolate.

Remove the foil from the pastry case and fill the case with the chocolate mixture. Bake in the now low oven for about 60-70 minutes. The filling might still be slightly 'wet' when removed from the oven. Don't worry: because of its retained heat it will continue to cook after removal.

LISTENER'S RECIPE

CHOCOLATE NOUGAT CANDIES

MAKES 15

A VERY PROUD *Mrs Sheila Bennett from Essex sent me this recipe, with which her daughter Jayne won a children's cookery competition when she was only 13.*

INGREDIENTS

90 g (3½ oz) good-quality chocolate, broken into pieces
1 tablespoon golden syrup
1 tablespoon clear honey
50 g (2 oz) seedless raisins, chopped into small pieces
50 g (2 oz) porridge oats

TO DECORATE
4 glacé cherries, chopped, or blanched almonds

Melt the chocolate in a bowl placed over a pan of boiling water. Put the syrup and honey in with the chocolate and when the mixture is smooth and runny, mix in the raisins and oats. (If you keep the bowl over the saucepan of water you will help to keep the mixture smooth.) Now divide the mixture between the paper sweet cases and leave to set before topping with the cherries or almonds.

CHRIS WALKER'S RADIO 2 CHRISTMAS TRUFFLE COLLECTION & FESTIVE RECIPES

Chris Walker first came on *The Debbie Thrower Show* after he successfully bid to do so at our annual Radio 2 Children in Need auction. We discovered that Chris is in fact the chef and proprietor of the Creebridge House Hotel in Dumfries and Galloway. Since then, he has come back to the programme a number of times to present some of his wonderful recipes for us. Here, he shares some of his own Christmas recipe ideas as well as the Radio 2 Christmas Truffle Collection, which he created especially for the show.

THE RADIO 2 CHRISTMAS TRUFFLE COLLECTION

SARAH'S SOFTY MARSHMALLOW SURPRISE

INGREDIENTS

200 g (7 oz) white chocolate
200 g (7 oz) marshmallows
**110 g (4 oz) glacé cherries,
each cherry cut in half**

YOU WILL NEED

cocktail sticks
small bowl
pan
*large sheet of silicone paper
or wire cooling rack*
paper sweet cases

THIS IS A *delicious white-chocolate-coated marshmallow with a glacé cherry centre.*

Melt the chocolate in the bowl over a pan of boiling water and then remove it from the heat. With a sharp knife, make a small incision in each marshmallow and push a cherry half inside each one. Using a cocktail stick to hold each marshmallow and cherry in position, dip the bottom half of the mallow into the melted chocolate, then put on the silicone paper (or a rack) and allow to cool until the chocolate is set. Then place it in a paper case.

TERRY'S TIPSY TRUFFLE

INGREDIENTS

150 ml (5 fl oz) double cream
300 g (11 oz) good-quality milk chocolate
1 teaspoon instant coffee powder
2-3 tablespoons Irish whiskey
empty solid chocolate shells
cocoa powder, to dust

YOU WILL NEED

pan
sieve
piping bag and nozzle
paper sweet cases

MADE WITH *Irish whiskey, this is a delicious mix of chocolate and coffee rolled in cocoa.*

Bring the cream to a boil in the pan and add the chocolate and the coffee. Remove the pan from the heat and beat everything lightly until the chocolate is melted. Now add the whiskey, stir thoroughly and leave, covered, to cool overnight in the refrigerator.

The following day, either pipe the mixture into the empty chocolate shells and dust each one with the sieved cocoa powder before placing it in a paper case, or roll the mixture by hand and then roll in the cocoa powder to coat before placing in the paper case.

KEN'S HIGHLAND THING

INGREDIENTS

200 ml (7 fl oz) double cream
300 g (11 oz) good-quality dark chocolate, broken into pieces
2-3 tablespoons Drambuie chocolate vermicelli

YOU WILL NEED

pan
paper sweet cases

A DARK CHOCOLATE *and Drambuie truffle rolled in chocolate vermicelli. Try these in your sporran!*

Bring the cream to boil in the pan and then add the chocolate. Remove the pan from the heat and beat the mixture lightly until the chocolate is melted. Add the Drambuie, stir well and then leave, covered, to cool overnight in the refrigerator.

Next day, roll out small balls of the mixture and coat each one in the vermicelli before placing it in a paper case.

J.Y.'S MALIBU AND COCONUT TRUFFLE

INGREDIENTS

200 ml (7 fl oz) double cream
300 g (11 oz) good quality bitter chocolate, broken into pieces
1-2 tablespoons Malibu
75 g (3 oz) desiccated coconut

YOU WILL NEED

pan
paper sweet cases

C LOSE YOUR EYES *and dream of those beaches favoured by Jimmy when he's on holiday.*

Bring the cream to boil in the pan and then add the chocolate. Take the pan from the heat and beat lightly until the chocolate is melted. Now add the Malibu and half of the coconut. Cover the pan and allow the mixture to cool, covered, in the refrigerator overnight.

Next day, roll out the mixture into small balls and then roll each ball in the remaining desiccated coconut before placing each truffle in a paper case.

DEBBIE'S DELIGHTFUL ORANGE TUILE

INGREDIENTS

100 g (4 oz) icing sugar
25 g (1 oz) unsalted
  butter, melted
25 g (1 oz) plain flour
40 ml (1½ fl oz) orange
  juice
50 g (2 oz) flaked almonds
finely grated zest
  of ½ orange

YOU WILL NEED

mixing bowl
non-stick flat baking tray
wooden spoon

A LITTLE CRISP *tuile biscuit with a hint of orange - a dainty little number.*

Mix all the ingredients together in the mixing bowl. Divide the mixture into 16 equal teaspoonfuls and place these on the baking tray. Refrigerate for an hour. Meanwhile, pre-heat the oven to 425°F/ 220°C/gas 7. After the hour is up, flatten each spoonful of mixture with the back of a spoon to form discs. Bake in the pre-heated oven for 3-5 minutes until they are golden. Remove from the oven and allow to cool a little before removing and folding the tuiles over the spoon handle. Leave to cool completely before removing.

LISTENER'S
RECIPE

SPICED ORANGE TEA

MAKES 1 300 ML (10 FL OZ) MUG

INGREDIENTS

orange peel tea, lemon
  peel tea, cinnamon tea,
  in three equal parts to
  taste (usually 1 heaped
  caddy spoon of the
  mixed tea per mug)
3 tablespoons orange
  juice
2 tablespoons ginger
  cordial

B EING PARTIAL TO *a good cup of tea, I was very interested to try this recipe for a mug of tea which Mrs Elizabeth Young sent me from Cambridge.*

Make up the tea in a pot and allow it to brew for at least 4 minutes. Place the orange juice and the ginger cordial in the pan and heat. Pour into the mug before adding the strained tea.

ED'S ALMOND CALORIE ACCUMULATOR

INGREDIENTS

75 g (3 oz) caster sugar
50 g (2 oz) flaked
almonds
120 ml (4 fl oz) double
cream
100 g (4 oz) bitter
chocolate, broken into
pieces
cocoa powder, sifted

YOU WILL NEED

2 pans
shallow tray or baking dish
small clean hammer or toffee
hammer
sieve
paper sweet cases

THIS CRUNCHY *almond and caramel truffle is a test for anyone.*

Gently melt the sugar in a saucepan, over a low heat, stirring constantly. Keep a constant eye on the saucepan as the sugar will burn quickly if you aren't careful. As soon as the sugar has turned to a golden-brown caramel, remove the pan from the heat. Add the almonds to the caramel and then pour it into a shallow tray to cool. (It will look like a nut brittle when it is.)

In another saucepan, bring the cream to the boil and add the chocolate. Take the pan off the heat and beat the mixture lightly until all the chocolate is melted. Allow the mixture to cool slightly before removing it from the tray and smashing it into small pieces with the hammer. Then fold the pieces into the chocolate mixture. Roll the mixture into rounds and then roll each one in cocoa powder before placing it in a paper case.

LISTENER'S TIP

I HAD TO INCLUDE *this hangover cure from Brian Turner in Hampshire, just in case you might need it...*

Splash three or four squirts of Angostura Bitters into a glass, top up with 200 ml (7 fl oz) of soda water, drink it and go to bed!

HOT PECAN AND WALNUT PUDDING WITH BUTTERSCOTCH SAUCE

SERVES 4

INGREDIENTS

FOR THE PUDDING
4 large eggs, separated
175 g (6 oz) caster sugar
50 g (2 oz) walnuts,
  chopped
50 g (2 oz) pecan nuts,
  chopped
juice and zest of 1 large
  orange
100 g (4 oz) self-raising
  flour

FOR THE SAUCE
100 g (4 oz) unsalted
  butter, softened
100 g (4 oz) demerara
  sugar
25 g (1 oz) plain flour
300 ml (10 fl oz) milk

YOU WILL NEED

2 mixing bowls
20 cm (8 in) square or
  round cake tin
silicone paper or baking
  parchment
pan

I F YOU FANCY *the stodgyness of Christmas pudding but just can't face the raisins and fruit, then this pudding is a real winter warmer. Finished with butterscotch sauce, it is delicious.*

PRE-HEAT THE OVEN TO 350°F/180°C/GAS 4. LINE THE CAKE TIN, GREASING IF NECESSARY.

First make the pudding by beating the egg yolks with the caster sugar in a mixing bowl until thick. Then add the nuts along with the orange zest and juice and mix well. Carefully stir in the flour. In a separate bowl, whisk the egg whites until stiff and then fold them into the pudding mixture. Turn the mixture into the cake tin and bake in the pre-heated oven for 45 minutes.

To make the sauce, beat the butter, sugar and flour together gently in a pan over a low heat. Leave the pan on the heat until the butter melts and the mixture begins to bubble. Cook the mixture for 4 minutes, stirring continuously. Now stir in the milk and bring the mixture to the boil, stirring until the sauce is thick and smooth.

Serve the pudding hot with the sauce poured over.

DARK CHOCOLATE, HONEY AND WHISKY SOUFFLÉS

SERVES 8

INGREDIENTS

unsalted butter, for greasing the dishes
2 level tablespoons caster sugar, plus enough for dusting the ramekins
225 g (8 oz) good-quality dark chocolate, broken into pieces
300 ml (10 fl oz) single cream
1 tablespoon whisky
1 tablespoon clear honey
5 large eggs, separated

YOU WILL NEED

8 ramekin dishes
bain-marie or dish placed in a roasting tin of boiling water
pan
mixing bowl
whisk

THIS DARK-CHOCOLATE *soufflé has a fine Scottish flavour as it combines whisky with honey - a true hot toddy.*

GREASE THE RAMEKIN DISHES WITH THE BUTTER AND DUST EACH ONE WITH A LITTLE CASTER SUGAR. PUT TO ONE SIDE. PRE-HEAT THE OVEN TO 350°F/180°C/GAS 4.

In a pan over a low heat, melt the chocolate in the cream, stir well and allow to cool. Now beat in the whisky, honey, the remaining caster sugar and the egg yolks, one by one. In a separate bowl, whisk the egg whites until they form stiff peaks and then fold them into the chocolate mixture. Divide the mixture between the ramekin dishes and place them in the bain marie or equivalent. (Make sure the water is boiling when it is poured into the bain-marie and that it reaches two-thirds of the way up the sides of the ramekins.)

Bake in the pre-heated oven for about 25 minutes and serve in the ramekin dishes.

ECCLEFECHAN TART

SERVES 6-8

INGREDIENTS

FOR THE PASTRY
175 g (6 oz) plain flour
75 g (3 oz) unsalted butter
1 large egg, beaten

FOR THE FILLING
50 g (2 oz) unsalted butter
225 g (8 oz) sultanas
2 large eggs
50 g (2 oz) demerara sugar
2 teaspoons white wine
vinegar

YOU WILL NEED

mixing bowl
rolling pin
20 cm (8 in) flan tin with
removable base
pan

D EBBIE DESCRIBED *this as 'little hand grenades of flavour' as she discovered the plump sultanas baked with butter, sugar, eggs and, my secret ingredient, vinegar, set on a shortcrust pastry base. Serve it for a Christmas afternoon tea or as an after-dinner pudding - delicious with ice-cream.*

PRE-HEAT THE OVEN TO 350 F/180°C/GAS 4.

First make the pastry by rubbing together the flour and butter until it looks like fine bread-crumbs. Mix in the egg to make a stiff dough. Roll out the pastry and then line the flan dish with it.

To make the filling, melt the butter in a pan and add the remaining ingredients. Stir well and then pour the mixture over the pastry case. Bake for 35 minutes or until golden brown and set.

Delia & Simon's Phone-in Top Tips

M arjory Graham from Cambridgeshire was worried about her Christmas pudding which she had kept since the previous year. It was in a glass dish, wrapped with a cloth, but had shrunk and was dry. Delia advised it's best to remove the cloth, make little holes all over the top and pour over a tablespoon of brandy before wrapping the pudding in a clean cloth or greaseproof paper and then foil. (Don't let the foil make direct contact or the fruit will react.) Then steam for two hours on the day.

PAT CHAPMAN'S SPICY IDEAS FOR CHRISTMAS FOOD

However much your family and guests tuck in to Christmas lunch, there always seems to be a large quantity of turkey left over. Most of us have our own tried and trusted recipes for using up the meat, but we thought that it would be a good idea to ring the changes with some new ideas. So we invited along Pat Chapman, who is well known to our listeners as the founder of the Curry Club, to spice up our taste buds with his more exotic gastronomic delights for left-overs as well as recipes for festive occasions.

THAI RED SOUP

SERVES 6

INGREDIENTS

3 tablespoons soya or sunflower oil
1 teaspoon garlic purée
1 teaspoon ginger purée
1 teaspoon paprika
½ teaspoon chilli powder
1 teaspoon bottled Thai red curry paste (optional)
200 ml (7 fl oz) tinned coconut milk
1-2 lemon grass stalks, if available
4-5 lime leaves, fresh or dried, if available
½ red pepper, cut into thin strips

THIS SPICY SOUP can equally suit vegetarians (who should omit the chicken stock cube and shrimps) or non-vegetarians, either to start a meal or to accompany rice or noodles. It makes a splendid pre- or post-Christmas party dish, being quick and simple to make.

Heat the oil in the wok. Stir-fry the garlic and ginger for about 30 seconds. Add the paprika and chilli powder along with the curry paste, if you are using it, and stir-fry briskly for about 20 seconds. Now add the coconut milk, mixing it well. When it comes to a simmer, add the lemon grass and lime leaves, if available, and the red pepper chillies (if using) and radishes. Continue to simmer for 3-4 minutes. Meanwhile, dissolve the stock cube in a

59

1-2 red chillies, shredded (optional)
6 radishes, quartered
1 vegetable or chicken stock cube
600 ml (1 pint) boiling water
100 g (4 oz) cooked shrimps (optional)
100 g (4 oz) bean sprouts (optional)
2 tablespoons fresh basil, chopped
soy sauce, to taste
freshly ground black pepper

YOU WILL NEED

wok or large frying pan
jug or bowl

jug with the boiled water. Now add the stock to the wok along with the shrimps and bean sprouts, if you are using them. Simmer for a further 3-4 minutes. Add the basil and the soy sauce. Serve immediately, piping hot, garnished with a twist of black pepper to taste.

CRUSTY OLIVE BREAD

SERVES 4

INGREDIENTS

freshly-baked baguette, still warm
olive oil
good-quality olives, stoned (you can use black or green ones)
freshly ground black pepper

YOU WILL NEED

serving dish

DELICIOUS SERVED *at a party, this is the perfect accompaniment to Cajun Black Chilli Chicken (see page 63). I got this idea from my grandmother's Anglo-Indian cookery book, which was first published in Calcutta in 1877. Olive oil and olives were status symbols in the pantries of the Raj!*

Take the baguette and, with a very sharp knife, cut a slit into it. Anoint the bread with olive oil, stuff it with top-quality olives and season with freshly ground black pepper. Serve in slices (or you could buy the individual baguette-style rolls that some supermarkets stock these days and make individual olive breads).

TURKEY PULLAO RICE

SERVES 2

INGREDIENTS

150-200 g (5-7 oz) cooked turkey pieces
4 tablespoons vegetable oil
1 teaspoon garlic purée
1 teaspoon ginger purée
3-4 teaspoons curry paste
4-6 spring onions, bulbs and leaves chopped
2-4 cupfuls cooked plain or use a flavoured rice of your choice
salt to taste
fresh coriander and/or mint, to garnish

YOU WILL NEED

wok or large frying pan

DESPITE BEING *the founder of the Curry Club, I still stick to the traditional turkey Christmas lunch with all the trimmings. On Christmas Day evening I love turkey sandwiches, spread with Indian pickle, but I'm still left with a significant amount of cooked turkey left-overs for Boxing Day. This really simple, quick to cook, rice-based spicy recipe has a dual function. It uses up the left-overs and supplies the curryholic with a post-Christmas fix!*

Remove the skin, bone and any unwanted matter from the turkey. Cut the meat into bite-sized pieces. Heat the oil in the wok and then stir-fry the garlic, ginger and curry paste for a minute. Now add the spring onions and continue to stir-fry for a further minute. Add just enough water to stop the sizzling in the wok. Toss in the turkey pieces and stir-fry everything for 2-3 minutes. Finally add the rice and salt the dish to taste. Continue stir-frying until everything is completely hot. Garnish the dish with the herbs and serve immediately.

If you have large quantities of turkey left over, you can freeze this dish, but you must do so before adding the rice. Defrost thoroughly before heating through in the wok again and then continue the recipe as before.

CHILLI BUBBLE AND SQUEAK

SERVES 2

cold roast/baked/boiled
  potatoes
cold peas, diced carrots,
  and/or sweetcorn
cold Brussels sprouts
gravy
stuffing
3 tablespoons vegetable
  oil
1 teaspoon garlic purée
2-3 fresh green chillies,
  shredded
4-5 spring onions
bread sauce, bacon,
  sausages, chestnuts
  (all optional; use if you
  have them to hand), cut
  into small pieces
salt and freshly ground
  black pepper
fresh basil, to garnish

YOU WILL NEED

potato masher
wok or large frying pan

THIS IS MY OTHER *Boxing Day recipe, which uses up the potatoes, vegetables, gravy, stuffing and accompaniments such as bread sauce, bacon, sausages and chestnuts. I've not given measures of the left-overs. Judge them by what you have to hand and your hunger.*

Chop and then mash the potatoes. Add the peas, carrots, and/or the sweetcorn if you have any available. Finely chop the Brussels sprouts and add these with the gravy, stuffing and any other left-overs listed. Heat the vegetable oil in the wok or equivalent. Stir-fry the garlic, chillies and spring onions for about 3 minutes. Add the bubble and squeak mixture and stir-fry everything until very hot. (Make sure you keep stirring or the ingredients will start to stick to the wok.) Season to taste and then serve immediately, garnished with the basil.

CAJUN BLACK CHILLI CHICKEN

SERVES 4

INGREDIENTS

1 teaspoon ground
coriander
1 teaspoon ground cumin
2 teaspoons paprika
½ -1 teaspoon chilli
powder, to taste
2 teaspoon garlic powder
1 teaspoon white pepper
1 teaspoon yellow mustard
powder
1 teaspoon curry powder
(optional)
4 skinned and filleted
chicken breasts, each
weighing about
150-200 g (5-7 oz)
sunflower oil, for coating
the chicken

TO SERVE
soy sauce
lemon wedges

YOU WILL NEED

ribbed skillet pan or a
barbecue
shallow bowl (a casserole lid
would do)
knife
pastry brush

THIS CAJUN CHICKEN *is the business and you will certainly find it in the Louisiana Bayou. You might like to try serving it as part of an alternative pre- or post-Christmas dinner or party menu. It is really simple and relatively quick to prepare and cook. Using chicken breast with a spicy coating creates a lot of smoke, so it may be best to save it for summery barbecue days. But who wants to wait for the summer? Serve it with Crusty Olive Bread (see page 60) and a dressed fresh salad.*

START HEATING YOUR SKILLET OR PREPARE AND LIGHT THE BARBECUE.

Mix the spices together in the shallow bowl, keeping them dry. Using the knife put small gashes into each side of the chicken breasts (this helps them to retain more coating). Brush the breasts with the oil, then dip them into the spice mixture, ensuring they are evenly and liberally coated. Cook the chicken breasts on the skillet or the barbecue. Turn each breast after about 5 minutes and cook for at least 5 minutes more (this will depend on how hot the skillet or barbecue is when you start). It is important to check that the breasts are cooked right through by cutting into the centre of each one: the meat should be white right through. Serve the chicken as described in the introduction with soy sauce and lemon wedges.

FIONA HUNTER'S
CHRISTMAS FOOD HYGIENE

With so many food scares around these days, the last thing you want to have to worry about at Christmas is whether or not the food you are serving your guests is safe. We went along to speak to Fiona Hunter, nutritionist of *Good Housekeeping Magazine*, to ask her expert advice on exactly how we should handle turkey, both before and after cooking, and the best way of coping with a bulging fridge full of food. Here is what she told us.

FOOD HYGIENE AT CHRISTMAS

With the festive season in full swing, food hygiene is probably the last thing you have time to think about, but following a few simple guidelines will help to ensure that your Christmas is not only a happy one, but healthy too.

Basic food hygiene, such as washing your hands before preparing food and then again in between handling raw and cooked foods and making sure that work surfaces and equipment are kept scrupulously clean is important throughout the year. But at Christmas time – with fridges and freezers crammed full to the brim and lots of extra mouths to feed – good food hygiene is more important than ever. On top of basic food hygiene, during the festive season, there are a few areas that require special attention.

TURKEY TIPS

Thawing

Frozen turkeys can be kept for up to six months in the freezer, which means that you can avoid the last-minute panic that is often part and parcel of shopping at Christmas. Frozen birds are also more economical to buy than fresh. However, if you are buying a frozen bird, do make sure you allow enough time to thaw it properly. Frozen turkeys that haven't been completely thawed are a major cause of food poisoning at Christmas. Thawing a large bird can take

Spice up your Christmas fare with Pat Chapman's recipes which can be found on pages 59-63. Try Thai Red Soup, Turkey Pullao Rice, and Cajun Black Chilli Chicken with Crusty Olive Bread. And for a spicy decoration make Stephanie Donaldson's Shaker Garland from page 84.

*I always think that a traditional Christmas lunch is hard to beat.
You'll find my own family's favourites (some traditional, others more
unusual) on pages 22-37.*

Get into the party spirit with Chris Walker's delicious Party Nibbles (pages 122–125) served with Mulled Wine (pages 17 and 44). Stephanie Donaldson's table decorating ideas (page 88) are simple but will impress your guests.

Mary Berry puts the icing on the Christmas cake (pages 10,11 and 14) and tempts us with Christmas Brandy Ice-Cream Pudding (page 18) and he Very Best Shortbread (page 20). Chris Walker's Radio 2 Truffles and Orang Tuiles (pages 51-54) would make a delicious present.

Giving presents you've made yourself is extra special.
Stephanie Donaldson's wonderful ideas for aromatic gifts
can be found on pages 98–106.

much longer than you might imagine – a 11.25 kg (25 lb) turkey will take over 48 hours to thaw. (Check the chart below for full advice on thawing times.)
🦃 The best place to thaw a turkey is in a cool room. Remove the plastic wrapping and cover loosely with greaseproof paper or a plastic bag. Check the bird regularly and remove the giblets as soon as they are loose. As soon as the bird has completely thawed – the legs should be flexible and there should be no ice crystals remaining in the cavity – place it on a large plate, cover it loosely, and transfer it to the bottom of the fridge. Once your turkey has thawed it can be kept in the refrigerator for up to two days.
🦃 Thawing in the microwave is not recommended.

THAWING TIMES			
Frozen Weight	Thawing time	Frozen Weight	Thawing time
2.5 kg/5½ lb	20 hrs	9 kg/20 lb	48 hrs
4.5 kg/10 lb	22–24 hrs	11.25 kg/25 lb	48+ hrs
6.75 kg/15 lb	24–28 hrs		

Stuffing
🦃 Always stuff the neck of the bird rather than the cavity. Stuffing the main cavity makes it difficult for the heat to penetrate and so there's a danger that the stuffing won't be cooked adequately. Allow about 225 g (8 oz) stuffing for each 2.5 kg (5½ lb) dressed weight of bird. Pack the stuffing loosely into the neck just before cooking.

Cooking
🦃 To calculate the cooking time weigh your turkey after it's been stuffed. Calculate the complete cooking time so that the bird is ready 30 minutes before carving; this allows 'resting' time for the flesh to firm up, making carving easier.
🦃 To cook, spread the skin with a little butter or margarine, season with salt and freshly ground black pepper, cover loosely with foil and place in a pre-heated oven, 190°C/375°F/gas 5. As a general rule, for birds 6.75 kg/15 lb and under allow 20 minutes per 450 g/1 lb, plus an extra 20 minutes. For birds over 6.75 kg/15 lb allow 15 minutes per 450 g/1 lb, plus an extra 15 minutes.

Baste regularly during cooking and remove the foil about one hour before the end of cooking to allow the skin to brown.

To check that your turkey is cooked properly, pierce the thigh with a skewer - if the juices run clear, the turkey is ready. If they're pink then it needs to be cooked for longer.

COOKING TIMES

Weight	*Cooking time*	*Weight*	*Cooking time*
2.5 kg/5 ½ lb	1¾- 2hrs	9 kg/20 lb	5½ -6½ hrs
4.5 kg/10 lb	3¼ -3 hrs 40 min	11.25 kg/25 lb	7+ hrs
6.75 kg/15 lb	4½ -5 hrs		

SAFE STORAGE

Because your fridge and freezer will probably be fuller than normal, and you may well be opening and closing the door more often than usual, it's worth checking that both of them are working at the correct temperature. To check, place a fridge thermometer in the middle of the top shelf, wait for a few hours then check the temperature: if it's above 5°C the fridge is too hot and you need to reduce the temperature. Your freezer should not be above -18°C.

Always allow hot food to cool completely before putting it into the fridge. Placing hot food directly into the fridge will cause the internal temperature to rise above 5°C.

Always keep cooked and raw foods on separate shelves in the fridge. Place raw foods, especially meat which may 'leak' blood, at the bottom of the fridge, and cooked foods at the top. Make sure that food is well covered.

LEFT-OVERS AND REHEATING

Any left-overs should be cooled as quickly as possible, covered and placed in the fridge. Left-overs should be kept for no longer than two days.

If you are re-heating food make sure you re-heat until it's 'piping hot'.

Never re-heat food more than once.

Any left-over turkey should be removed from the carcase and stored in the fridge or freezer. If you wish to re-heat left-over meat, cut into slices, cover with gravy and re-heat in the microwave or a conventional oven. Turkey slices covered with gravy can be kept in the freezer for up to one month.

PARTY PREPARATION THOUGHTS

When cooking for crowds, as is often the case at Christmas, it can be best to avoid certain foods.

Raw eggs The current advice from the Department of Health is that because of the risk of salmonella, we should not eat raw eggs or uncooked food made using them - such as home-made mayonnaise, mousse, and ice-cream.

Soft cheeses Because of the risk of listeria, pregnant women should avoid mould-ripened soft cheeses, such as Brie and Camembert, and blue-veined cheese, such as Stilton. Hard cheeses, cream cheese, cottage cheese, cheese spread, fromage frais and yoghurt are all safe to eat. Pregnant women should also avoid meat, fish or vegetable pâté, unless it is canned or marked as pasteurised.

Nuts Although nut allergy is not particularly common, the reaction is severe and in some cases can prove fatal. People with nut allergy will react to even the minutest quantity. If you're catering for a large group of people it may be safer to avoid using nuts and any products, for instance nut oils or peanut butter, that are made from them.

MARTIN WARD'S
CHRISTMAS WINE SELECTION

M ost of us are confident about our choice of Christmas food, but how many of us loiter anxiously in front of the rows of wine at the supermarket, confused and bewildered as to what will suit our turkey or goose, or pudding, best? Well, Martin Ward, who runs the Heart of England School of Wine, certainly doesn't, which is why we asked him to give us the benefit of his advice on selecting the best Champagne and wines to serve with your festive fare.

F rom what people say to me, I'm beginning to believe that there is no more emotive subject, in matters of wine, than choosing what to serve with Christmas lunch. I'm often asked how much a good bottle of wine will cost, or if Hungarian wine is as good as French or Australian. Or, 'What differences does a grape variety make?' Well, if you've had a few wine disappointments in the past, this year should be more succcesful and delicious than before.

I've included here wines that you should be able to find in high-street wine merchants and supermarkets. When you make your own selection, bear in mind that, even if you follow one grape variety, you may get surprises (nice and not so nice), as the taste and style of a grape can vary according to the wine's origin, wine-making techniques, and the maturation period and method. Remember that just seeing the name of a favourite grape on the label is no guarantee that you will like the wine.

CHOOSING A BOTTLE OF FIZZ

If you fancy serving an aperitif on Christmas Day it's hard to beat a good Champagne, but the sky can be the limit on price. Some supermarkets have good-quality own-brand Champagnes. And there are some wonderful 'traditional method' sparking wines about. In France, the little-known Savoie is home to Varichon et Clerc. Or try Quartet by Louis Roederer. In Australia, Moët et Chandon produce Green Point. All are worth considering.

TEMPERATURE

Serve chilled and not frozen to allow the flavour to come out. I'm sure you don't really need me to tell you to open the bottle carefully and serve immediately. Pour only a small amount into each glass at first, as the wine will continue to bubble and rise up in the glass after you pour. You can top each one up afterwards.

CHOOSING WINES FOR SERVING WITH TURKEY AND GOOSE

Both of these meats have a lot of flavour and richness, so any wine that is served with them needs to be able to balance this. You can, of course, serve either white or red wine, or both, depending on your own preference.

WHITE WINES

The style of the perfect white wine should be somewhat robust with lots of flavour and richness to give enough taste and decent acidity to cut through the food flavours. People often confuse fruit and sweetness in white wines. In a dry white, the fruit needs to be present to balance the necessary crisp acidity that gives life and lift to the wine. The sweetness should come from the residual, or added, sugar in the wine, which is, of course, added at different levels, according to the type of wine. Some people prefer a very dry white wine, others a fruity dry white and, when drunk with the right thing (for example your Christmas pudding, see page 71), some of the sweetest white wines can be thoroughly enjoyable.

Chardonnay This is currently a very fashionable wine and two I would suggest are Gallo Sonoma Chardonnay from the eponymous valley in California, and the Rosemount Estate Chardonnay from the Hunter Valley in New South Wales. Both of these wines have bags of flavour and, while oak-matured to a degree, have a lovely balance that suits turkey or goose.

Sauvignon Blanc A classic that is well worth considering. My favourite is still a well-made Sancerre or Pouilly-Fumé from the beautiful Loire Valley in France. Look out for a Pouilly-Fume by Fouassier in Tesco or Sancerre La Vigne des Rocs in Asda - both of them are classic 'old-style' wines. If you fancy something from the New World try Boschendal Sauvignon Blanc Grande Cuvée from the

Cape vineyards of South Africa. Or consider Sauvignon Blanc from Phillipe de Baudin. This is produced at Domaine de Baume in the Languedoc of Southern France but by BRL Hardy of Australia, so it combines the best of both worlds.

Riesling This grape has a great acidity and lots of fruit. Try *trocken* (dry) Mosel and Rhine Rieslings, from the estate of Ernst Loosen and Dirk Richter.

TEMPERATURE

In this country, there is a great tendency to serve white wine far too cold. As a result, all the subtle flavours are killed and all you can taste is – well, cold. White wine should be chilled not frozen! Pop the bottle in the fridge, or leave it in a cool place for about half an hour, and open the wine just before serving.

RED WINES

Don't forget that some of the younger oak-aged wines may have huge tannins (that's the stuff that leaves your mouth feeling furry when you swallow some wine) and may need time to mellow. The tannin is what gives the wine its structure and life so that it harmonizes with the food flavours. If you drink a 'big' red wine on its own you'll feel the tannin. But drink the same wine with a meal (say a venison casserole) and it will taste softer and less aggressive on the palate. The acidity in a red wine, which in a poor wine can make your eyes water, is what gives it longevity and helps to balance the tannin and, hence, the taste.

Cabernet Sauvignon Look out for good-quality wines being produced from Hungary, Australia, South Africa and Chile. A good estate is Klein Constantia from South Africa and, from the same country, look out for the Neethlingshof Estate Cabernet. The Santa Carolina vineyard in Chile is also producing some first-class wines.

Cabernets are often blended, and the Australians do this with great success. For a special bottle that is hard to beat, try Cabernet Merlot of Chateau Reynella.

Shiraz A grape very much at home in Australia – in fact it is the most important red grape by far in that part of the world. It has a spicy taste and is an ideal match for meat. The Australian Rosemont vineyard is a name to look out for. And, again, look out for Klein Constantia Shiraz from the Cape vineyards in South Africa.

Zinfandel This is a versatile grape and some of the best examples are robust wines such as Gallo Sonoma Zinfandel.

Tempranillo A wonderful grape that you may not have heard of, but will have tasted in most Riojas. Seek out a bottle of Reserva or Gran Reserva from one of Rioja's top vineyards such as La Rioja Alta, Faustino or Marqués de Murietta. These are oaky wines that mature on release and taste smooth, fruity and subtle.

TEMPERATURE

Just as we often serve our white wines too cold, we worry too much about warming our reds. We are usually told to serve red wines at room temperature but, in fact, your own room temperature at Christmas is likely to be 70-75°F (21-24°C), which is really too hot. An ambient temperature is what you need to take the chill off and soften the hard facets of one of the wines listed above.

Opening the bottle an hour or two before the meal will not allow the wine to 'breathe' enough. You'd be better to transfer the wine to a clean bottle and back, or to a decanter in order to aerate the entire contents. Some older reds will need decanting anyway to remove natural but unsightly sediments. It's best to do this carefully through a clean muslin cloth.

CHOOSING WINES TO SERVE WITH PUDDINGS

Puddings need a powerfully flavoured wine with substantial sweetness that is never cloying or treacly. You'll only need a small glassful - so it's rather handy that you can often buy these wines in half-bottle sizes.

Muscat This grape variety is often ideal and needn't be expensive - try Moscatels de Valencia or the Muscat from the Greek island of Samos (available from Majestic Wine Warehouse).

Riesling Yes, its that grape again. For dessert Riesling, look out for the later harvest version of Auslese, Beererauselese, and Trockenbeerenauslese. Kirch-heimer Schwarzerde Beerenauslese offers particularly good value.

TEMPERATURE

Serve dessert wine well chilled.

ADAM PASCO'S CHRISTMAS FLOWERS & CHRISTMAS TREE GUIDELINES

There is something rather special about having beautiful, scented flowering bulbs and house plants in the home over the festive period. Perhaps it is something to do with reminding us that, despite the long, cold winter nights, spring is not that far away. I have always found it rather hit and miss to get poinsettias and hyacinths looking at their best when the house is full of people on Christmas Day - somehow looking after the plants often falls to the bottom of my list. When I asked the advice of Adam Pasco, the editor of *BBC Gardeners' World Magazine*, and our regular gardening expert on the programme, how I could make the most of all things green and floral in the house over Christmas, he had masses of ideas that I thought you'd like to share. From choosing and preserving Christmas trees, to keeping house plants at their peak for next December, and planting bulbs in autumn, Adam has given us the benefit of his considerable knowledge.

BUYING POT PLANTS FOR CHRISTMAS

Millions of pot plants are sold each Christmas, with seasonal favourites like poinsettia, azalea, cyclamen, solanum and Christmas cactus at the top of the list. Here is some timely advice about buying them:

🌺 Buy your plants from a nursery or store that really cares for their plants. It is often a false economy to buy cheaply from very cold, windswept street markets, as the plants may be damaged before you even buy them.

🌺 Once plants like cyclamen receive a cold shock they will almost certainly turn up their toes as soon as you get them home. Make sure that plants are fully wrapped or enclosed in a plastic sleeve before taking them from the store to your car, and aim to get them home as soon as possible.

✼ If you buy plants in advance as gifts, then unwrap them when you get home and stand them in a cool but bright position. Remember to water them if the compost is dry.

✼ Most flowering pot plants will last longer if grown on the cool side. Keep them away from fires and radiators, and also draughts caused by doors and windows. Keep their compost just moist and they will provide colour for many weeks beyond Christmas.

✼ If the plants are already in flower in the store, remember to check to see how many more flower buds are still to come. If flower production is too advanced, then the display will soon be over, so choose plants that have plenty of flower buds still to open. This is easy to see on an azalea, but with cyclamen you will have to delve deep down to the base of the leaves, as new flowers grow up from the top of the tuber.

CHRISTMAS HOUSE PLANTS AND THEIR CARE

POINSETTIA

These offer great value for money and last for months. The flowers at the very tips of each shoot are actually quite insignificant, as it is the surrounding modified leaves, or bracts, which colour up in autumn to provide the show. The traditional red poinsettia is still the most popular, but varieties with pink and cream bracts are also available. As a rough guide, prices are usually about £1.00 per bract, but very large plants will be charged at a premium. In recent years, the big supermarkets have sold good-quality plants very cheaply, so look out for poinsettia bargains when you are doing your shopping.

When you get the plants home, keep them in a warm and well-lit position, away from radiators and draughts: they need a minimum temperature of 55-61°F (13-16°C). Allow their compost to almost dry out between waterings, and feed weekly with a liquid house-plant fertilizer. Their colourful bracts will then reward you with a long-lasting display.

Aftercare Once the plants look a little tired, cut them down in spring to leave shoots just a few inches long. New shoots will develop during spring and summer. Commercial growers have access to dwarfing growth regulators but, as we gardeners don't, you may well find that your plants will now grow taller than the original plant.

Colour for next Christmas To encourage flowering and coloured bracts to form, the plants need to be subjected to carefully controlled lengths of day and night. Poinsettia only flower if they receive a long, dark night followed by a short day. In the home, lights going on and off at night prevent this happening. To get round the problem, get a large cardboard box or black bin liner that will fit right over the plant. From late summer or early autumn, put this over the plant every teatime and leave it in place to give the plant a 14-hour night, removing it to give it a 10-hour day. Repeat this treatment for at least eight weeks, and flowering should be initiated. There is no need to continue this treatment for any longer, and your poinsettia can now be placed on a warm, bright windowsill to develop its full colouring. You can also take cuttings from the new growth in early summer - treat the newly rooted plants in the way described above.

AZALEA

These lovely evergreen flowering plants can last for many years if treated correctly. Many are potted in terracotta rather than plastic pots, so stand them on a saucer of gravel that is kept constantly moist with rain water. Azaleas hate hard water, which contains lime (it causes their leaves to turn yellow), so collect rain water or use water from a dehumidifier. This is one plant whose compost should never be allowed to dry out. Keep azaleas in a cool position of around 50-61°F (10-16°C) in good light.

Aftercare After flowering, pick off the dead flowers. Keep the plant well watered and fed right through the year. If plants appear pot-bound, re-pot them in spring into large pots using an ericaceous compost.

Colour for next Christmas Some people stand their plants outside in a shaded site for the summer, bringing them back indoors in early autumn before the weather turns cold. Plants should flower again during late autumn and winter.

CYCLAMEN

Buy plants that have plenty of flower buds still to come. Cyclamen like it cool - around 50°F (10°C) is best - and quickly keel over in very hot rooms. They should also be grown in full light, as they get drawn and lanky under poor light conditions. Always water cyclamen from below, standing pots in a small saucer of water. Never soak the compost, but water a little every few days. Over-watering can cause the tuber and roots to rot.

Aftercare Faded flowers should be removed by holding their stalks tightly and then twisting and pulling sharply. Continue feeding and watering until June or July, and then withhold watering, letting the compost dry out and foliage die down. Stand the pot somewhere it can bake, such as on a sunny bedroom windowsill or greenhouse shelf.

Colour for next Christmas By October you should see new leaves developing from the top of the tuber. Watering can gradually be resumed, and plants should be grown on in a cool, bright position. Only repot cyclamen when absolutely necessary, as plants can be left growing, undisturbed, in the same compost for many years, providing they are fed.

CHRISTMAS CACTUS

The exotic shrimp-like blooms of *Schlumbergera truncata* provide valuable winter colour over many weeks, usually in shades of pink. This plant offers great value, getting bigger and carrying even more bloom every year. As with all cacti and succulent house plants, it is important not to over-water them. Keep plants in a bright position, and stand in a saucer of water for an hour once a week, allowing the plant to take up what it needs before throwing away the excess.

Aftercare Pick off dead flowers regularly. If blooms are left to dry on the plant for a week or two they come away easily. Water plants with a liquid feed each week during spring and summer to encourage new growth, but reduce watering in the autumn. Keep the cacti in full light, preferably on a south-facing windowsill, through the summer. Small plants that look unstable or pot-bound should be potted into larger pots using a compost with extra grit added to improve drainage. Tall terracotta pots are best, as they are more stable, more difficult to over-water, and allow the stems to spread and trail beautifully.

Propagation tips Leaf sections root easily in gritty compost to form new plants. Cut off a leaf section about 7.5 cm (3 in) long in summer, putting three or four in a small terracotta pot. Roots develop from the region between leaf sections, and new growth quickly forms from the tips.

Colour for next Christmas Plants will come into flower again next Christmas on their own. Keep them in good light during the autumn and you should notice flower buds forming at the very tips of every leaf. Avoid moving plants unnecessarily or standing plants in draughts, as this can lead to bud-drop.

FLAMING KATY

The succulent *kallanchoe* produces a fine display of flower heads carried above its deep-green, fleshy foliage. Pink, orange and red flowers are common, but a new pure white is now available. Care is similar to that for the Christmas cactus, keeping plants in full light, but ensuring temperatures never drop below 50°F (10°C). Allow the compost to dry out slightly between waterings.

Aftercare Cut off faded flowers, following the flower stalk down to just above the first pair of large leaves. This usually encourages new leaf shoots to develop. Large plants can be pruned harder back to generate new growth. Water sparingly, adding a liquid feed during spring and summer. Repot into fresh gritty compost each spring.

Propagation tips New plants can be raised from short stem-cuttings in summer, or even from individual leaves. Simply break these carefully from the parent plant and insert the cut end into gritty compost.

Colour for next Christmas The shortening days of autumn and winter naturally trigger flowers to form. Artificial lights in the home can disrupt flower initiation, so keep plants on the windowsill in a spare bedroom to avoid lights coming on at night. Once flowers can be seen, plants can be moved back to a bright windowsill so that you can enjoy their flowering display.

AMARYLLIS

Hippeastrum bulbs make a wonderful Christmas gift. Once planted in a warm position, the large bulbs send up one or two thick shoots topped by several brightly coloured trumpets of bloom that last for many, many days. Bulbs are sold by size, so larger bulbs will cost a little more than small ones. Most are sold in picture boxes in supermarkets and department stores, and while some are ready planted, others come with a pot and compost for you to plant at home. Full instructions should be provided, but the key to success is a warm position providing a temperature of at least 61°F (16°C), and good light when in growth. Turn the pots daily once in growth to prevent shoots bending towards the light. Tall plants in flower can also become top heavy, so stand the plant pot inside a decorative ceramic container for extra support.

Aftercare After flowering, cut the old flower stem right down to its base and keep watering the plant and feeding it each week. Keep it on a warm windowsill for the summer, and gradually withhold water so that the compost dries out completely for a few weeks. Amaryllis are an evergreen bulb, and although their foliage may remain green, it could die down. If it does, cut it off just above the top of the bulb. Start watering again in late autumn to encourage plants to flower again.

HANDLE WITH CARE!

The winter cherry, or *Solanum capsicastrum*, is covered with attractive colourful ornamental fruits. Some look like shiny orange sweets, so do keep these plants away from young children. The berries can be harmful if eaten.

If the stem or leaf of a poinsettia is damaged it can exude a sticky, milky, white sap. Avoid getting this on your hands or skin when handling plants as it can cause an itching allergic reaction in some people.

Fragrant hyacinths can fill the room with their intoxicating perfume during winter, especially if prepared hyacinth bulbs were planted in August to produce early blooms. Contact with hyacinths can cause an allergic reaction on the skin, so either wear gloves when handling the bulbs or plants, or wash your hands thoroughly after touching them.

BUYING THE BEST CHRISTMAS TREE

More than five million real Christmas trees will be sold this year and, if news from the British Christmas Tree Growers Association is anything to go by, there is no shortage of excellent quality trees to choose from. Prices for cut trees of the traditional Norway spruce are around £10-£15 per 2 metre (6 ft 6 in) tree, but the trend towards non-needle-drop varieties continues. These are more expensive, perhaps costing around £25 or more for a quality Nordmann or Noble fir of a comparable height.

All Christmas trees need water, whether they have roots or not. Cut trees should be treated rather like cut flowers, with the base of the trunk positioned in a reservoir of water that can be topped up each day. Just because a variety claims to be non-needle drop does not mean it doesn't need water and, although needles are slower to drop with these varieties, they will stay healthy for longer if regularly watered. For this reason it is often best to avoid buying trees whose cut stem is pushed into a wooden block for support. Instead, choose a fresh tree, and shake it vigorously to ensure needles are not already falling. If they are, leave it alone and choose another, or shop elsewhere.

BUYING A CHRISTMAS TREE TO LAST

For just £3-£4 more than a cut tree you can buy trees that have been dug up and root-balled. Some growers even sell trees that have been grown in pots throughout their life. Take care, though, as some growers simply pull trees from the soil and push them into pots with a little compost. These have not been pot-grown, and are unlikely to survive in the long run. A pot grown tree could be an excellent investment, as a living tree can be grown in a large pot of loam-based John Innes No 3 compost, and, if well cared for, can last for many years.

It is usually best to choose a reasonably small tree, and to check the roots before you buy. Provided it has a good root system, pot it up right away, keeping it well watered and in a sheltered position outside. Living trees will not tolerate several weeks of warm conditions indoors, so either find a cool spot for your tree, such as a porch, or keep it outside until the last minute and use as a decoration for just a few days over Christmas before taking it back outside. In this way, your investment will grow each year, but remember that the tree will need regular watering and feeding during the growing season, and occasional re-potting in future.

Garden centres sell a wide variety of pot-grown conifers, both of traditional types of Christmas tree and a host of other varieties with gold, green and blue foliage. Some of these could be brought indoors and decorated for Christmas before returning to the garden and grown as a container plant.

CHOOSING AND CARING FOR YOUR CHRISTMAS TREE

🌲 For the freshest trees, buy home-grown trees direct from the grower or look for the tree and Union Jack symbol of the British Christmas Tree Growers Association (12 Laviston Road, London SW19 4 TQ, telephone 0181 946 2695). British-grown Christmas trees will be far fresher than imported trees. Some growers open their fields and allow you to choose in situ.

🌲 To lengthen the life of the tree, aim to keep it outside or in a very cool position until close to Christmas. Roots should be kept moist, or cut ends stood in a bucket of water. Mist with water daily. .

🌲 Always shake the tree thoroughly before bringing it into the home, and give it a good brush. This removes loose needles and dirt or soil that may be trapped in the branches. If the foliage looks soiled, wash the tree down with a hose and stand it outside to dry.

🌲 Prepare the site to receive your tree, covering carpets with a large sheet or mat to collect any needles that may fall. Once Christmas is over, simply lay the tree down on the sheet and roll it up so that it can be carried from the house without leaving a trail of debris behind it.

🌲 Wear gloves when handling Christmas trees, as they produce a very resinous, sticky gum that is hard to wash off. Some varieties, such as the Blue Spruce, have quite vicious sharp needles, so gloves are essential when handling them.

🌲 With sawn trees, re-cut the base of the stem once you get it home, sawing off about 2.5 cm (1 in) of wood. This opens up the channels in the trunk of the tree so that they will take up water.

🌲 Living Christmas trees need water, and a large tree can drink up to 600 ml (1 pint) of water a day. Stand the cut stump in water, either in a purpose-made Christmas tree stand, or in a bucket. Top up the water level daily.

🌲 Clamp trees firmly to hold them upright. Stands with built-in reservoirs are ideal, but an old bucket with bricks jammed in to secure the stem will work well. Avoid filling in around sawn trees with soil, as this can clog up the stem and prevent water uptake.

🌲 Trees with roots can be planted in buckets of moist sand or soil for support. Keep the soil moist throughout the Christmas period. Roots will have been badly damaged during harvest, so the tree is unlikely to survive afterwards.

🌲 Position the tree in a cool, bright position away from fires and radiators. Direct heat can quickly desiccate the needles so that they fall prematurely. The cooler the position, the longer your tree will look good.

🌲 With care, pot-grown trees can last many years. Keep these in the home for as short a time as possible. Water thoroughly before bringing indoors, and then water daily. Take back outside after Christmas and plant outside.

🌲 Needle-fast trees should not need treating with an anti-transpirant, but the traditional Norway spruce may benefit from being sprayed with a proprietary chemical made for this purpose. Some people claim that hair spray or lacquer does the same job.

BE SAFE AT CHRISTMAS! TAKE CARE WITH CHRISTMAS TREES

The needles of some varieties of tree are particularly sharp. Take care when handling trees, and ensure branches do not spread out across seating at eye level. Vacuum up needles daily to prevent pets or children injuring themselves. Both Christmas trees and their decorations can be highly combustible. *Never position a tree close to a fire or decorate it with candles.*

Check tree lights are in good working order, that plugs are sound, and that cables are not damaged. Discard damaged lights. If lights do not work, turn them off at the mains before removing bulbs. *Always consult a qualified electrician if you have problems with lights.*

AFTER TWELFTH NIGHT - RECYCLING OLD TREES

Even old Christmas trees have a value, as they can be shredded and recycled into bark mulch. Some nurseries accept back old trees to recycle, while most local tips will take trees to recycle, composting the wood chippings to use on flower beds and paths in your area.

THE CHRISTMAS TREE VARIETY GUIDE

NORWAY SPRUCE *Picea abies*

Established as the genuine Christmas tree, with branches that sweep upwards and short, soft, bright-green needles. Do make sure that the cut end of the stem is kept in a reservoir of water.

NORDMANN FIR *Abies nordmanniana*

This is a well-shaped tree, sometimes also called the Caucasian fir. The needles are flat, deep green, and grow out right round the shoots to provide a full, bushy appearance. Each needle has grey and green stripes on the underside. Needle retention is excellent, although not quite as good as the Noble Fir.

NOBLE FIR *Abies procera*

A wonderful Christmas tree, producing regular, tiered branches. Needles are blue-grey in colour, and sweep upwards along the shoots. This is the best tree of all for needle retention.

DOUGLAS FIR *Pseudotsuga menziesii*

An attractive aromatic conifer with long, slender, pale-green needles. A nice tree, but slimmer than the Norway spruce. Holds its needles reasonably well.

SERBIAN SPRUCE *Picea omorika*

Another nicely shaped tree with quite short needles, which are deep green on top and silvery grey below, providing a frosty appearance. Good needle retention.

BLUE SPRUCE *Picea pungens*

Makes a beautiful silvery blue Christmas tree, well branched with a good shape. Be careful as the needles are very sharp, so wear gloves when handling, and avoid if you have young children.

SCOTS PINE *Pinus sylvestris*

For a tree with a difference choose the Scots pine, which has branches clad in lovely long, twisted needles that will hang on all over Christmas.

STEPHANIE DONALDSON'S CHRISTMAS WREATHS, GARLANDS & TABLE DECORATIONS

Y ou know that Christmas truly has arrived when the decorations start to go up. Traditional wreaths have never been more popular than they are now, as wonderful variations on the age-old holly theme are being created by top florists. Stephanie Donaldson runs Christmas workshops at the Chelsea Physic Garden in London every year, so she was the expert we turned to for advice both on creating your own wreaths and decorating the lunch table speedily but sumptuously for Christmas Day. For more of Stephanie's ideas for aromatic presents and ways to scent your home, turn to page 98.

A FESTIVE WREATH FOR THE DOOR

O ne of the nicest things about taking a bit of extra care over the wreath on the front door is enjoying all the appreciative comments that greet you when you open the door to your guests. The wreath is a symbol to the outside world that you are celebrating the Christmas festival, and is the first sign of welcome to family and friends.

Most shop-bought wreaths tend to be fairly unimaginative, and it can prove difficult to add your own decorations, as they often feature quite a lot of very prickly holly. Professionally made wreaths are usually constructed from a wire ring to which moss and greenery is attached using florist's wire. For the inexperienced this is a fiddly process and can involve starting all over again if you aren't happy with the results. The easy alternative is to use a straw ring as the base, and pin the moss and foliage in place using wire pins. German pins are ideal and can be bought through flower-arranging clubs or florists' suppliers, or, alternatively, you can cut your own from medium-gauge florists' wire, which is widely available. The ring is prepared by covering it with a layer of moss and then pinning this into position. Refer to Figure 1 for guidance.

Nowadays there are many types of cut pine and fir available at Christmas time, but the best variety for a wreath is undoubtedly the blue pine. It is wonderfully fragrant, has a lovely silvery blue sheen and lasts a long time without dropping. Figure 2 shows it being pinned into position.

The choice of decorations for the wreath are really a matter of personal taste, but it's always a good idea to look around for fresh inspiration. Shops put up their decorations long before we do, and it's worth looking at what they are incorporating into their displays. Magazines are also a good source of inspiration, as are the windows of fashionable florists. Exotic fruits and vegetables are all the rage for wreaths at the moment, and you need look no further than the supermarket shelves for these. Providing they are not too soft they will last well on the wreath, although it is advisable to have a few extra just in case they start to look a bit sad or the local wildlife joins the feasting. Wired ribbon is now widely available and is perfect for bows on a Christmas wreath. The wire ensures that the bows keep their shape and that they don't droop in damp weather.

When adding any strong decorative feature to your wreath, such as the bows or groups of fruit, keep to odd numbers to ensure that the finished wreath looks well balanced. For instance it is far easier to position three or five bows on the ring, than two, four or six which require much more precision.

FIGURE 1

FIGURE 2

A SHAKER GARLAND

YOU WILL NEED

2 medium-sized oranges
baking tray with a wire rack
  inside
kitchen paper
bradawl or drill
6 cinnamon sticks
5 fresh red chillies
approximately 100 fresh
  bay leaves
75 cm (30 in) medium-
  grade garden wire
3 15 cm (6 in) lengths of
  tartan ribbon
small bundle of 50 cm
  (20 in) lengths of raffia

FIGURE 3

FIGURE 4

THERE IS SOMETHING *very appealing about Shaker style, particularly at Christmas time when the use of simple natural materials is a refreshing contrast to the over-decorated glitz that we see everywhere else. To make this garland you will need a source of fresh bay leaves because the dry ones are too brittle and will snap as you thread them on to the wire. The orange slices can be dried well ahead of the time when you plan to make the garland as long as they are stored in a warm dry place.*

Although you may be making the garland for Christmas, there is no need to take it down with the other decorations on Twelfth Night. Instead, hang it in the kitchen, where it will be a useful source of bay leaves throughout the year and, although the colours will fade gently, it will still look good right through to next Christmas. And then you can make another one!

1 To dry the orange slices, first pre-heat your oven to about 250°F/120°C/gas ½. Cut each orange into 10 thin slices and lay them on a wire rack above a baking tray lined with paper (to catch the juice).

2 Place the baking tray in the oven with the door very slightly ajar to allow the moisture to escape. Check the orange slices after 30 minutes: if they have started to brown, turn the oven down still further. They should dry in 1-2 hours depending on your oven.

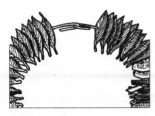

FIGURE 5

FIGURE 6

FIGURE 7

FIGURE 8

3 Remove the baking tray from the oven and place the rack in the airing cupboard or over a radiator for a couple of days to remove any residual moisture.

4 Now you should be ready to assemble the garland. Begin by using a bradawl or drill to make a small hole through the centre of each cinnamon stick. Refer to Figure 3.

5 Arrange all the prepared materials in separate piles.

6 Bend over one end of the wire to form a hook approximately 4 cm (1½ in) long. Refer to Figure 4.

7 Thread ten of the bay leaves onto the wire, followed by orange slices and another ten bay leaves.

8 Now thread one of the cinnamon sticks onto the wire and then tie a length of ribbon onto the wire next to the cinnamon stick before threading on a second cinnamon stick.

9 Follow this with ten bay leaves and a chilli. Thread the wire through the chilli's stem, where it meets the base of the chilli, and then thread another ten bay leaves.

10 Use the rest of the materials by repeating steps 7 to 9 twice more, and then bend the other end of the wire into a second hook, and hook it onto the first hook to form a circle (refer to Figure 5).

11 Make the raffia bow by taking a single strand of raffia and using it to tie the bundle of raffia strands together in the middle (refer to Figure 6). Then (Figures 7 and 8), form a loop from either end of the bundle and tie in the middle with the piece of raffia that secures the bundle. Trim the ends of the raffia to form neat tails and tie the bow onto the garland so that it conceals the wire hooks.

A RED-HOT WREATH

YOU WILL NEED

small brass or plastic ring
(the sort used for
Austrian blinds)
reel of fine florists' wire
30 cm (12 in) straw ring
length of ribbon or string
carpet moss, fresh or dry
medium length German pins
(4 cm / 1½in wire pins)
blue pine
9 long red chillies
small bag of fresh reindeer
moss
artificial holly berries
3 tartan bows

OPTIONAL EXTRAS

a few sprigs of Scots pine
twigs
metal Christmas decorations

A VIVID DISPLAY *of glossy red chillies at the super-market was the inspiration for this unusual but festive Christmas wreath.*

1 Before you do anything else it is advisable to fix the brass or plastic ring to the wreath to ensure that you have something to hang it by. There is nothing worse than completing the wreath and then trying to fiddle about at the back as you try to create a fixing without squashing your work of art (see Figure 9 for guidance). Cut a length of florist's wire and loop it through the brass or plastic ring, then position the ring on the back of the straw circle and fasten it in place by looping the wire through the small ring and around the straw two or three times.

2 Tie a length of ribbon or string to the small ring. This will prevent you losing it when you cover the straw with moss and will also mark the top of the wreath as you add the decorations.

3 Cover the straw completely with carpet moss, pinning the moss in place with the German pins.

4 Cut the blue pine into short lengths, no more than 10 cm (4 in) long and pin them onto the moss covered ring, working systematically round the ring until no moss is visible. Occasionally bend down and look at the wreath from the sides to ensure that there are no gaps around the edges,

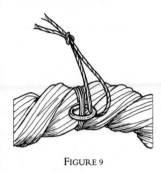

FIGURE 9

which will be much more obvious when the wreath is hanging on the door.

5 Position the wreath on the worktop so that the ring you are going to hang it by is central at the top.

6 Use the florist's wire to wire the chillies together in groups of three and pin them onto the wreath, positioning one at the base of the wreath and the other two opposite one another on the top half of the wreath.

7 Take a handful of reindeer moss and pin it in place around each of the groups of chillies.

8 Twist a small clump of holly berries round the centre of each of the tartan bows and pin the bows over the stem of the three groups of chillies.

9 If you wish, you can now add the sprigs of Scots pine, the twigs and the metal decorations, or any other finishing touches of your own choosing.

QUICK DECORATING IDEAS FOR THE CHRISTMAS TABLE

When it comes to decorating the Christmas table it's sensible not to let yourself get trapped into creating an elaborate and time-consuming centrepiece.

Keeping it simple doesn't mean that the table needs to look spartan, but rather that the decorations should be quick and easy to make. One of the most effective centrepieces is a group of small baskets, each filled with different seasonal fruits and nuts. Pile one high with golden kumquats or clementines, another with rosy red apples, a third with walnuts and a fourth with miniature pineapples. The pineapples are particularly appropriate, as they are traditionally considered to be a symbol of hospitality. This tradition dates from the days when the only pineapples available in Britian were those grown by the aristocracy in their hothouses, and sharing one with a guest was a gesture of great generosity. As a finishing touch, twine tendrils of ivy around the fruit-filled baskets and add some candles in pretty holders, and the centrepiece is complete.

If your table is too small for a centrepiece, you can still bring about a wonderful transformation by decorating the backs of the chairs. Trailing ivy, pine and holly can be tied into a seasonal posy, fastened with a generous tartan bow and tied or pinned onto the chair back. Add a few tendrils of ivy to the table top and tie each napkin with a tartan bow. The room will look festive without being cluttered.

LIGHTING THE CHRISTMAS TABLE

Candles are essential on the Christmas table, and if you have candelabra this is certainly the time to use them, but even if you don't you can still make your candles look special. Church candles are wonderfully proportioned and come in a variety of widths and heights. Instead of using them separately, tape three candles of different sizes together near the base and stand them in a terracotta flower pot filled with damp florists' foam. Push the candles firmly into the foam and surround them with fresh bun moss. For a warm, glowing light, stand small terracotta pots holding night lights in front of each place setting, but not if there are going to be small children at the table.

SALLY O'SULLIVAN'S GUIDE TO PRESENTS BY POST

On some Christmas shopping expeditions I seem to walk around for hours and yet come home with very few presents. When I was talking about this with Sally O'Sullivan, Editor-in-Chief of *Ideal Home* magazine, who regularly comes along to the programme, she came up with the perfect solution: to shop by post! Sally immediately drew up a long list of varied and exciting companies that have enticing catalogues full to the brim with original ideas for gifts in all price bands. We've included the list here for you to share, along with some sensible advice on your consumer rights as a postal shopper. So why not shop from your armchair this year?

PRESENTS BY POST

Mail-order shopping is now big business in the UK so look out for the specialist catalogues that could give you just the inspiration you need for those friends and relatives who already seem to have everything they could possibly want. There are catalogues now for virtually every hobby you can think of, from gardening to gliding.

The golden rule with mail-order shopping is to give yourself plenty of time. It's very unlikely that anything will go wrong, but if it does, you want to know you've got time to sort it out so that you can be sure you get your goods in time for Christmas. Always pay by credit card, if you can, then you won't lose out should something dire happen to the company you've ordered from – see Know Your Rights on page 97 for more advice.

The following is a selection of some of the most interesting and varied mail-order catalogues around:

ACCESSORIES

SUCCESSORIES

PO Box 4458, Henley on Thames, Oxon RG9 1EG, Dept. CL01

Tel: 01491 577056

Exclusive accessories and jewellery. Earrings from £14, scarves, belts, hats (fold-up hats approximately £60), bags up to £105, and sunglasses approximately £52.
P&P Varies per order
Payment All major credit cards

AROMATHERAPY

BOOKS

AROMATHERAPY ASSOCIATES LIMITED

68 Maltings Place, Bagleys Lane, London SW6 2BY

Tel: 0171 371 9878

A complete range of bath, body and facial oils, creams, and essences; grouped by body, mind, spirit or skin. These products were previously only available through selected health clubs, clinics and spas, and are renowned for their quality.

P&P £2 for one or two items, £3 for three

Payment All major credit cards

NEALS YARD REMEDIES

31 King Street, Manchester M2 6AA

Tel: 0161 831 7875

Extensive range of environmentally friendly, organic products to cleanse inside and out: Chinese and herbal tinctures, Bach Flower Remedies, essential oils, creams, cleansers, soaps and shampoos for the body, face, hair, and feet. An extensive range with prices varying from 60p-£25.

P&P £2.50, or, if total value of goods is more than £25, add 10 per cent

Payment All major credit cards

WATERSTONE'S

4-5 Milsom Street, Bath BA1 1DA

Tel: 01225 448595

A quarterly catalogue highlighting new launches - particularly good on new fiction and biography. You can be put on a specific-subject mailing list. Waterstone's Signed First Editions Collection is a no-commitment club offering signed first editions at retail price. Their catalogue offers over 150 titles each year and the annual subscription is £5.00.

P&P £1.25 for one paperback, £2.50 for two, £3 for all other books; free for orders over £35

Payment All major credit cards

DRINK

WINESHARE

Glebelands, Vincent Lane, Dorking, Surrey RH14 3YZ

Tel: 01306 742164
Fax: 01306 743936

A chance to be involved in wine making. WineShare allows you to rent a row of vines in a choice of two Appellation Contrôlée vineyards and then have the wine delivered to your door. (If you prefer you can collect the wine from the vineyard yourself.) Prices start at £50 (plus VAT) for annual rent of 50 vines up to £150

(plus VAT) for 150 vines. You can also taste before you rent: two bottles cost £13.50 (which includes post, packaging and insurance).
P&P Not applicable
Payment Cheque, Visa, Mastercard

ELECTRICAL

DIXONS DIRECT

PO Box 60, Hemel Hempstead, Hertfordshire HP2 7TZ

Tel: 0500 501050

Dixons' home electronics and communications brochure veers towards the hi-tech with a selection of personal organizers from £49.99, digital clocks, modems, desktop calculators, and security alarms, as well as televisions from £79.99, videos and stereo systems from £259.99.
P&P Depends on order
Payment All major credit cards

FOOD

THE OIL MERCHANT

47 Ashchurch Grove, London W12 9BU

Tel: 0181 740 1335

Oils (whether olive, nut or seed, organic, or flavoured with herbs or fruit) and vinegars (wine, balsamic, sherry or verjus). Extra virgin olive oils from Italy, Greece, France, Spain, and the USA (1 litre/1¾ pints from

£12.90). Oils made from walnuts, grapeseed, almonds, sesame (1 litre/1¾ pints from £6.45), and oils flavoured with truffles, mushrooms, basil and lemons (250 ml/8 fl oz from £3.50). Hand-made pastes and sauces include tuna, sardine and anchovy.
P&P Depends on the order
Payment All major credit cards

THE FRESH FOOD COMPANY

Freepost, 326 Portobello Road, London W10 5RU

Tel: 0181 969 0351

Supplying the hardest-to-find organic supplies. Fruit and vegetable boxes weighing around 6.75 kg (15 lb) cost £24.95. Cornish fish boxes are £56.95 and 'catch of the day' £47.95.
P&P Free
Payment All major credit cards

SWADDLES GREEN FARM

Hare Lane, Buckland St Mary, Chard, Somerset TA20 3JR

Tel: 01460 234387

Fine-quality English organic meat, poultry, pies, dairy produce, eggs, marinades, prepared meals, beers, and wines. Prices are very reasonable: beef £3.80 per lb, chicken £2.45 per lb, marinades £2.50 per pot, and a prepared meal of coq au vin £5.15.
P&P Depends on order
Payment Cheque, postal order

THE MOUSETRAP

2 St Gregory's Alley,
Norwich NR2 1ER

Tel: 01603 614083

A long and impressive list of British, Dutch, Danish, Norwegian, French, German, Italian, Spanish and Swiss cheeses. A few favourites are (prices per lb): Cheddars, oak-smoked, apple-wood, Rutland with beer, garlic and parsley, priced £3-£5.48; Wensley-dales from £3.40, and Stiltons from £4.00; the Scandinavian Danish Mycellas and Esrom Ambassadors from £3.50; Spanish manchego and Bruder basil-smoked from £4.48; Swiss Emmental and Gruyere both £4.96. Other products include meats, pâtés, olives and fish.
P&P Varies with item
Payment Cheque

TAYLORS OF OXFORD

31 St Giles, Oxford OX1 3LD

Tel: 01865 558853

Traditional hampers (from £25.95) and gift boxes (from £19.95), either in standard versions or made up to your own specifications. Wine boxes available from £20.
P&P Varies with item
Payment Cheque, postal order, Visa, Access

THE CLARK TRADING COMPANY

17 Southbrook Road,
London SE12 8LH

Tel: 0181 297 9937

Specializes in the most exotic food items from France and Italy: truffles, foie gras, extra virgin olive oils, vinegars and wild porcini mushrooms.
P&P Varies with item
Payment All major credit cards

MEG RIVERS CAKES

Middle Tysoe,
Warwickshire CV35 0SE

Tel: 01295 688101

Hand-made cakes with fresh organic ingredients. An extensive range: fruit (£11.50), cherry and ginger (£12.50) and wheat-free fruit cake (£13.50) are just a few. There are also made-to-order gift baskets from £12.50. Join the Cake Club for £83.50 per annum and receive six different cakes a year.
P&P £2.95
Payment Access, Mastercard, Visa, Delta, Switch

GAMES

PARLOUR GAMES

27 School Road, Bradenham,
Thetford, Norfolk IP25 7QU

Tel: 01760 440966

A husband-and-wife-run company that sells traditional board games

exclusively by mail order. Each game approximately £14.95.
P&P Free
Payment Cheque or postal order

GARDENING

ENGLISH GARDEN

PO Box 1030, Langley, Slough, Berkshire SL1 6BW

Tel: 0800 203000

Garden tools and equipment and a wide range of gifts for gardeners of all ages. From containers and ornaments, to tableware, stationery, bath and beauty products, to children's tools and toys. Highlights are a flower-pot salad bowl with matching aluminium garden-tool salad servers (£29.95 by Michael Updike) or flower-pot napkin rings in a rustic cardboard presentation box (£11.95 for 12).
P&P £3.95
Payment All major credit cards

HOME

THE HOLDING COMPANY

Mail Order, Unit 15, Imperial Studios, 3-11 Imperial Road, London SW6 2AG

Tel: 0171 610 9160

A substantial range of products designed to help you organize your home and life. Folding canvas storage

box from £13.95, woven hat boxes from £19.95, cedar shoe-care valet (£8.95), storage boxes from £8, jolly folding trolley at £16.95, and woven storage baskets from £6.95.
P&P £3.50, orders over £250 free
Payment All major credit cards

TURQUAZ

The Coach House, Bakery Place, 119 Altenburg Gardens, London SW11 1JQ

Tel: 0171 924 6894
Fax: 0171 924 6868

The Turquaz range of bedlinen and tablecloths, all 100 per cent natural fibre, available in sunny Mediterranean colours. Sheets start at £20 for a fitted single, duvet covers from £45 for a single, pillow cases from £12. Tablecloths start from £15, napkins from £10 for six, and place mats £14 for six.
P&P Free
Payment All major credit cards

THE WHITE COMPANY

298-300 Munster Road, London SW6 6BH

Tel: 0171 385 7988

Good-quality linen, towels, accessories for the bathroom, kitchen and bedroom, together with bone china seconds all in white. Bathrobes (£29.95), Irish linen damask napkins (£12.95), dinner plates (£4.95) and tablecloths (£16.95).

P&P £2.75; £4.75 for orders over £35
Payment All major credit cards

KNOBS AND KNOCKERS

567 King's Road,
London SW10 0LR

Tel: 0171 384 2884

Door and window furniture, as well
as cabinet and bathroom fittings,
fireside paraphernalia, and sundry gift
items are all available from this company. It sells Regency-style polished
brass door-knockers, bell-pulls and
handles, black iron latches, hooks and
hinges, china finger plates, keyhole
covers and mortice knobs.
P&P Depends on order
Payment All major credit cards

MᶜCORD DESIGN BY MAIL

Blagrove, Swindon,
Wiltshire SN5 8SN

Tel: 01793 433499
Fax: 01793 487002

A company which offers a wide
range of furniture, crockery, and
accessories for the home at affordable
prices. Six recycled wine glasses
£24.99, 20-piece Chinese dinner set
£19.99, sofas from £299, wrought
iron mug tree £12.99, and a beech
desk from £125.
P&P £3.50; orders over £100 free;
upholstered furniture £25
Payment All major credit cards

THE ART ROOM

Witney, Oxfordshire OX8 6BH

Tel: 01993 770444
Fax: 01993 700749

A selection of practical and highly
decorative objects for the home. Art
is the theme with framed prints by
Monet, works by David Hockney and
Alberto Morocco from £24.95, sterling silver Modigliani jewellery from
£9.95, a gold-plated steel Dali clock
£125, and an outrageous inflatable
'Scream' by Edward Munch £29.95.
P&P £2.95
Payment All major credit cards

MELIN TREGWYNT

Castle Morris, Haverfordwest,
Dyfed SA62 5UX

Tel: 01348 891644

Traditional blankets, made from 100
per cent pure new wool in timeless
vibrant primary colours, plaids and
checks, are produced in the Melin
Tregwynt studio. Prices start at
£15.50 for a 91 x 137 cm (36 x 54
in) pram blanket, to £75 for 152 x
183 cm (60 x 72 in) fringed throw.
Gift wrapping is £1.50 extra.
P&P £1.50 for orders up to £25;
£2.75 for orders up to £50; £4.75
for orders over £50
Payment All major credit cards

BRITISH TELECOM

In Touch, BT Freepost GW 7520, Glasgow G2 6BR

Tel: 0800 800150

In Touch magazine brings you the latest and best ideas from British Telecom. There is a vast range of telephones, answering machines and mobile phones, with helpful and flexible options on renting or buying.
P&P £2.99
Payment All major credit cards

CUSHIONS

Unit 6, 98 Victoria Road, London NW10 6NB

Tel: 0181 963 0994

An off-the-peg range in classic fabrics with a contemporary feel. These include raw silks, denim, chambray, gingham, ticking, and towelling. Cushions also offers a cushion couture service, designing, making-up and trimming to any specification. Prices start from £12.95; the couture service starts at £9.50, excluding fabric.
P&P Varies with item
Payment: Cheque, postal order

JEWELLERY

CHUNKYDORY

55 Cuckoo Hill Road, Pinner, Middlesex HA5 1AU

Tel: 0181 866 7263

Costume jewellery in silver, glass, gold, pearls and wood, both fun and elegant. Prices range from £2.50-£25.
P&P Varies with item
Payment Cheque and postal order

THE COACH STORE

8 Sloane Street, London SW1X 9LE

Tel: 0171 235 1507

Luxury leather accessories for men and women. All rather pricey, but top quality. Briefcases from £430 and belts from £175, pebble-textured leather bag at £250.
P&P Varies with item
Payment Cheque, postal order, and all major credit cards

WORTH JEWELLERY

PO Box 710, High Wycombe, Buckinghamshire HP13 5GT

Tel 01494 472271

Amber combined with sterling silver hand-crafted jewellery. Cufflinks for £41, amber studs from £8, pendants from £6.40, bracelets from £97 and necklaces from £10.
P&P £1.50
Payment Cheque and postal order

TIFFANY AND CO.

25 Old Bond Street, London W1X 3AA

Tel: 0171 409 2790

Features only the very best from exclusive designers. Phenomenally expensive – for under £100 you don't have much choice: a purse pencil for instance. Jewellery starts at £305 for earrings, £3575 for a bracelet, and £57,000 for a sapphire ring.

P&P Depends on order

Payment All major credit cards

PETS

A. RAINBOW HORSE SUPPLIES

Bromley Mill, Bromley Road, Congleton, Cheshire CW12 1PT

Tel: 0260 273771

Traditional designs combining good performance and long-lasting quality. The range covers exercise sheets (£28), rugs (from £44), and machine-washable quilts (from £35). Also a range of warm and waterproof hard-wearing, lightweight outdoor clothes for country pursuits such as fishing, riding and shooting from £35.

P&P Varies with item

Payment All major credit cards

CATAWARE

Victoria Mill, Bakewell, Derbyshire DE45 1DA

Tel: 01629 813 993

A collection of 1000-plus themed items for you and your cat. Items range from cat care, home wares, jewellery, stickers and stamps, gifts

and games, toys and books. Prices start from as little as £2.50.

P&P Varies with item

Payment All major credit cards

THE BONES DOG AND CATALOGUE

The Upper Mill, Coln St. Aldwyns, Cirencester GL7 5AJ

Tel: 01285 750007

An exclusive range of necessities and accessories to accommodate your cat or dog. All types of bedding (from £15.99), collars and leads (from £7.50), a range of toys (from £5.00), plus natural and homeopathic remedies. Also car-seat covers and grooming kits.

P&P £3.25–£7.50 depending on order

Payment All major credit cards

KNOW YOUR RIGHTS

In case anything goes wrong you need to be aware of your rights.

Make sure you buy from a reputable and established business. A well-presented catalogue and a knowledgeable voice on the end of the phone are good signs of a legitimate and organised business.

Make sure the catalogue or the publication in which the advert appears is current, and always read the conditions of purchase.

✈ Always check the conditions for returning goods and refunds. Mail-order goods can generally be returned if they are sent back within the time specified by the company, in the original packaging and in pristine condition. Faulty or damaged goods should be exchanged or refunded.

✈ Check that the company is a member of one of the mail-order organizations such as The Mail Order Traders' Association (Tel: 0151 227 4181), which is for larger mail-order catalogues. If a registered company advertising in the main national papers defrauds you, or goes bust, you can request a refund directly from the Mail Order Protection Scheme (MOPS), 16 Tooks Court, London EC4A 1LB. The Periodical Publishers' Association, Imperial House, 15-19 Kingsway, London WC2B 6UN, is a similar organization that vets companies advertising in magazines.

✈ Always keep the brochure or a copy of the advertisement that relates to the goods you've ordered, and a record of how you paid (e.g. make a note of your cheque number). Never send cash in the post.

✈ If your order is for a large amount of money, send it by recorded delivery. Goods should be delivered within a reasonable amount of time – up to 28 days is normal for most companies.

✈ If you're dissatisfied with your products, always contact the company in writing and explain what is wrong. Say where you saw the advert and the date that it appeared. Give full details of the goods ordered, the amount and method of payment, and the date that you made your order. The more information you give the better and keep a copy of everything.

✈ If you do have a problem with mail-order goods, your local Citizens' Advice Bureau can help. If you feel the advert for the goods was false, or misleading, write to the Advertising Standards Authority, 2 Torrington Place, London WC1E 7HN.

✈ 'Buying by Post' is a helpful leaflet available from the Office of Fair Trading, Room 310C, Field House, 14-25 Breams' Buildings, London EC4A 1PR (Tel: 0171 242 2858).

STEPHANIE DONALDSON'S AROMATIC GIFT IDEAS

Stephanie Donaldson is a very talented lady who knows not only about crafts, but flowers and aromatherapy as well. We always have a massive response every time she appears on the programme. When Stephanie told us how to make these wonderfully aromatic gifts we were inundated with requests for written instructions. Fortunately, Stephanie, who is the author of a number of books, was happy to let us have them. Here she suggests ideas for gifts for cooks and for anyone who appreciates being pampered, as well as ways to create a Christmas atmosphere in the home with the fragrances of essential oils. Look out for her table-decorating ideas on page 88 and her fabulous wreaths on page 82.

GOOD ENOUGH TO EAT

Edible gifts are always very welcome at Christmas, especially ones like these flavoured oils and vinegars, which can be used to give simple foods a delicious extra dimension.

SOME WORDS OF CAUTION

When making flavoured oils and vinegars it is very important that the bottles, corks and stoppers are clean and sterile. The easiest way to do this is to put them in the dishwasher and let it run through a cycle, or, alternatively, you can sterilize them in the traditional way in a pan of boiling water or in the oven.

RASPBERRY VINEGAR

MAKES 750 ML (1¼ PINTS)

INGREDIENTS

600 ml (1 pint) red wine vinegar
1 tablespoon pickling spice
450 g (1 lb) frozen raspberries
sprig of fresh lemon thyme

YOU WILL NEED

pan
bowl
sieve
unbleached coffee filters
clean and sterile bottles
   (see note on page 98)
labels
funnel

THIS IS QUICK and easy to make and can be used to make wonderful salad dressings, add piquancy to sauces, and can even be lightly sprinkled over soft fruits to bring out the flavour. Keen cooks would love a bottle of raspberry vinegar as a present, especially if you include some suggestions for using it on the label. Be sure to make a bottle for yourself - it's too delicious to give it all away.

Flavoured vinegars should be used within three months, so make sure that you write the date that you made it on the label.

1 Gently heat the vinegar and pickling spice in a pan for 5 minutes.

2 Pour the heated vinegar and spice mixture into a bowl containing the raspberries and the sprig of lemon thyme.

3 Cover the bowl and leave the mixture to infuse for 2 days. Stir occasionally.

4 Strain the vinegar through a sieve to remove the raspberries, thyme and spices and then strain the vinegar through a paper coffee filter to remove the fine sediment.

5 Pour into clean, dry bottles and seal with a cork or the original bottle top, which you have cleaned and sterilized thoroughly. Label the bottles.

GARLIC OIL

MAKES 900 ML (1½ PINTS)

INGREDIENTS

25-30 plump garlic cloves
900 ml (1½ pints)
  cold-pressed virgin olive
  oil

YOU WILL NEED

pan
unbleached coffee filters
funnel
clean and sterile bottles
  (see note on page 98)
labels

THIS IS ANOTHER delicious gift for cooks, especially cooks in a hurry who love the flavour of garlic, but can't always be bothered with the business of cleaning the garlic press each time they cook. The cloves are removed from the oil before bottling, and they are superb spread on slices of crusty baguette or used as a relish with grilled fish or meat. Store them in the fridge in a sealed jar, covered with a little oil and use within 10 days.

The bottled oil will keep well for three months if kept cool so make sure you date the label on the bottle.

1 Peel the garlic cloves – the easiest way to do this is to top and tail each clove with a sharp knife and then press down firmly on the clove with the flat edge of the blade. The skin will then come away without difficulty.

2 Gently heat the oil to a simmer in the pan. Do not let it boil or it will spoil the nutty flavour of the oil.

3 Add the garlic cloves and poach them in the oil for about 25 minutes until they are tender.

4 Remove the pan from the heat and leave it to cool completely.

5 Now remove the cloves and strain the oil twice through the coffee filters to remove any residues.

6 Using the funnel, pour the oil into clean, dry bottles, seal with clean stoppers and label.

SAFFRON OIL

MAKES 250 ML (8FL OZ)

INGREDIENTS

250 ml (8 fl oz) light olive oil
a large pinch of saffron strands (approximately 2 g / ¹⁄₁₆ oz)

YOU WILL NEED

small pan
2 120 ml (4 fl oz) bottles (see note on sterilizing on page 98)
funnel
labels

SAFFRON HAS ALWAYS *been valued as one of the most precious of spices and here it has been infused in oil ready to use as a very special flavouring for grilled fish. Decant the oil into small bottles and gift wrap each with its own basting brush.*

This oil is best used within three months, so again you would be best to add the date that you made it to the label.

1 Gently warm the olive oil in the small pan, add the saffron and simmer very, very gently for 5 minutes.

2 Remove from the heat and allow it to cool in the saucepan.

3 Pour the oil into scrupulously clean bottles, seal with new corks or stoppers and label.

4 Leave the oil to infuse for 2 weeks, shaking the bottles occasionally. The oil will then be ready to use.

SOME MORE WORDS OF WARNING

Although flavoured oils and vinegars look very attractive when whole herbs and flavourings are included in the bottles, recent research suggests that these can grow harmful moulds, especially once the bottles have been opened. For this reason it is recommended that they are removed once their flavour has passed into the oil or vinegar.

FRAGRANT CREAMS, LOTIONS AND TALCS

Although it is possible to make lotions, creams and talcs from scratch it can be a rather messy and time-consuming process that you probably won't want to get involved with in the hectic run-up to Christmas. The easy, and very successful, alternative is to buy some of the unscented body-care products sold in supermarkets and chemists and add fragrance by using pure essential oils bought from chemists or health-food stores.

The different oils vary enormously in price, depending on how complicated they are to harvest. Most of those used in these projects are inexpensive to buy or, where an expensive oil is recommended, a cheaper alternative is also suggested.

> *Please note: Essential oils are highly concentrated and when undiluted should be handled with care, especially if you have sensitive skin.*

PEPPERMINT BODY LOTION

INGREDIENTS

**10 drops of peppermint oil
175 ml (6 fl oz) unscented body lotion**

YOU WILL NEED

plastic bottle (see note right)
label

THIS IS AN IDEAL *gift for the sports enthusiast, who will appreciate a bottle of this refreshing lotion to use after sports or a strenuous workout at the gym. In this instance, a plastic bottle is the most practical container, so look in the shops for brightly coloured plastic bottles with a pump action for easy use. Peppermint oil is very powerful, so don't be tempted to add more than the recipe recommends, or it may cause skin irritation.*

Don't use on small children, or during pregnancy.

1 Drip the oil into the lotion and shake thoroughly to mix.
2 Decant into the bottle of your choice and label as appropriate.

SOOTHING SCENTED HAND CREAM

INGREDIENTS

10 drops camomile oil
5 drops lemon oil
5 drops lavender oil
120 ml (4 fl oz) unscented handcream

YOU WILL NEED

mixing bowl
pot
label

CAMOMILE, LAVENDER *and lemon oils are all good for the skin and here they are blended into an unscented handcream to make a lightly perfumed cream that will be pleasant to use as well as gently healing. A perfect present for a gardener, it could be given on its own in a lidded terracotta pot or in a box with a bar of soap, a nailbrush and a hand towel for a complete handcare kit.*
Avoid using camomile oil in early pregnancy.

1 Add the oils to the cream and mix thoroughly.
2 Decant into a decorative container and add a descriptive label.

DELIGHTFUL DUSTING POWDERS

INGREDIENTS

10 tablespoons fragrance-free talc
2 tablespoons cornflour
10 drops of the essential oil of your choice

YOU WILL NEED

2 mixing bowls
label and ribbon to tie it

THERE IS SOMETHING *wonderfully luxurious about dusting oneself liberally with fragrant talc, especially when a down powder puff is used. Fragrance-free talc is easy to find and, with the addition of a scented oil, it can be personalized with a favourite fragrance. The richest of all fragrances are rose and jasmine and they make wonderful dusting powders, but both these oils are very expensive to buy and you may prefer to use geranium instead. Its spicy fragrance is rich but not cloying and it makes a delightful dusting powder that is appreciated by young and old alike.*

When giving talc as a gift look out for 1950s glass and china powder bowls in antique markets, junk shops and car-boot sales where it is still possible to buy them quite cheaply. Alternatively, glass sugar shakers make original and practical containers.

1 Carefully spoon the talc into a bowl.

2 Spoon the cornflour into a separate small bowl and add the essential oil. Blend the oil thoroughly into the cornflour with a teaspoon and then add the cornflour to the talc and mix well - but be gentle or it will fly all over the place.

3 Decant into your chosen container and tie a label to it. Allow 10 days for the fragrance to mellow before you use the talc yourself or give it as a gift.

CREATING THE RIGHT ATMOSPHERE

So much of what we feel about Christmas is linked to childhood memories of cooking and baking with fragrant spices, the scent of orange peel and the resinous aroma of fir, spruce and pine, which were all part of the celebrations. There is something so wonderful about the smell of the home at Christmas that each year we find ourselves full of happy anticipation. Even if all your Christmas food is bought ready-made off the supermarket shelves, and there is more warming up than cooking and baking, and the Christmas tree came out of the loft, it is still possible to fill the house with the characteristic fragrances of Christmas with the help of a few essential oils.

On the next few pages you will find some simple but effective ideas to make for your own home, as well as for gifts.

CINNAMON STICKS

ALTHOUGH CINNAMON *sticks look wonderful in Christmas decorations they actually add very little fragrance because the characteristic aroma isn't released until the cinnamon is powdered. One way to overcome this problem is to sprinkle the sticks with cinnamon oil and seal them in a jar for at least a week to allow the fragrance to permeate through the sticks. They can then be used to add fragrance as well as texture to your Christmas decorations.*

Cinnamon oil is a skin irritant so wear rubber gloves when handling the treated cinnamon sticks.

INSTANT SCENTED CANDLES

ALTHOUGH YOU WON'T *be able to give these candles as a gift, they will be a perfect treat for you. Their aroma will conjure up happy memories and fill the air with a truly festive fragrance.*

Avoid cedarwood oil during pregnancy and handle cinnamon oil with care, as it can irritate the skin.

1 Blend the oils together in the dropper bottle.
2 Allow two weeks for the different fragrances to blend together and mellow before use.
3 To use, light the candles and trim back the wicks to ensure a small flame that will not vaporize the

oils too quickly. Once a pool of wax has formed around the wick, blow out the candle and drip 5 drops of the oil into the wax. Don't try to drip the oil onto the lighted candle, as the oil will burn and smell unpleasant. Re-light the candle and the room will quickly fill with the fragrance, which will linger in the air for at least an hour.

SCENTED PINE CONES

INGREDIENTS

120 ml (4 fl oz) lukewarm water
25 drops pine or cedarwood oil
pine cones

YOU WILL NEED

large mixing bowl
rubber gloves
cling film
newspaper
wooden bowl or basket
small bottle with stopper

A LARGE WOODEN *bowl or basket filled with pine cones looks suitably festive at this time of year and when the cones have been scented with pine oil they fill the room with their fragrance all through the holidays. These would also make a lovely gift.*

Avoid cedarwood oil during pregnancy.

1 Pour the water into the mixing bowl and add the essential oil.

2 Add the pine cones to the water and, wearing the rubber gloves, toss the cones in the water and oil mixture until they are all well coated.

3 Cover the bowl with cling film and leave it to stand in a warm place for a couple of days, stirring occasionally.

4 Remove the cones from the bowl and stand them on some newspaper in a warm place to dry.

5 Display in a pretty wooden bowl or basket. Keep any left-over water and oil mixture in a bottle to refresh the scent when it begins to fade.

CHILDREN & CHRISTMAS

ENTERTAINMENTS

For most of us, children help to make Christmas the magical time that it is. But, having said that, once school is out, it can be difficult to keep excited children amused and cheerful during the last few days before the 25th. No matter how well behaved your children or grandchildren may be under normal circumstances, the thought of all of those intriguing parcels bearing gifts for them can often be too much to keep them tame for long. My own experience, and that of friends and colleagues, has shown that the way to help maintain happiness and peace all round is to plan a few outings and to have a stash of amusements to keep them busy. Whether you are catering for four or 40, you'll be feeling pushed for time over the holiday period, so you'll need to be able to give children things they can do on their own, with a minimum of supervision, which either won't make any noise at all or very little! So, here's a checklist of things for you to consider having 'up your sleeve'.

A BOX OF 'TRICKS', INCLUDING

colouring pens, crayons, and pencils
paper-cutting scissors
an assortment of paper scraps
  including coloured paper
pieces of card
Christmas card templates to colour in
scraps of wool and fabric
large 'blunt-ended' sewing needles
old newspapers
paper glue (buy solvent-free glue
  made especially for children)
sticky tape
paperback books
talking books
last year's Christmas cards
old photographs
empty egg boxes
bubble wrap and shredded paper
board games
tape player with in-built microphone
  and blank tapes
videos

AND HERE ARE SOME IDEAS OF WHAT YOUR CHILDREN CAN DO WITH THEM

If the children need ideas about what to draw, suggest they make their own personalized Christmas cards and gift tags. If you've got some paper big enough, they could even have a go at designing their own wrapping paper.

Older children can be given scraps of wool and some aida (this is the fabric used for cross-stitch, which has holes in it ready for stitching) to do their own cross-stitch pictures. Suggest they cross-stitch some snowflakes which are relatively easy.

Good old-fashioned paper-chain paper is still available from stationers and craft shops. Give the children some, or get them to make their own from scraps, and ask them to decorate the hall with paper chains.

Books are a marvellously quiet pastime for children of all ages. Either encourage your children to visit the local library to pick up some reading material for the holidays or buy some cheap paperbacks throughout the year and produce them, magically, at the start of the holiday. You know your own children's tastes but try a mixture of fiction, joke books, craft books, comics, and colouring books. You could also try talking books - see my present ideas on page 111 for more information.

Last year's Christmas cards can be made into gift tags.

Unwanted photographs (make sure they don't get to your treasured snaps!) can be made into amusing personalized cards and collages. A large collage of family photographs (even if they are of poor quality) can make a wonderfully unusual present for a grandparent or godparent.

Make junk models with egg boxes, bubble wrap and shredded paper.

Dust off those old board games. They are perfect for the cold, dark days.

How about getting the children to record their own radio programme? Get them listening to BBC Radio 2 first to inspire them and then they can have hours of fun being amateur disc jockeys!

Videos are always worth considering if you get desperate!

OTHER HOME ENTERTAINMENT IDEAS ARE

If they are old enough, ask the children to decorate the Christmas tree but under no circumstances should you let them near the lights. Always supervise this activity though - children falling off wobbly chairs would not make a good start to Christmas!

Have you ever wondered why it is that children are full of energy before Christmas but, as soon as you try to get them to write their thank-you letters afterwards, they somehow run out of it? It's just possible that you could persuade older children to start writing their thank-you letters now, leaving the relevant bits blank for filling in later. Cannier children may understand your intentions so it could be worth a try!

Get cooking. Ideal recipes for children can be found on page 113.

Suggest they clean out their bedrooms and toy boxes in anticipation of needing space because of the spoils they're hoping for from Father Christmas.

Set them up to play the party games on page 119.

IDEAS FOR OUTINGS

A family trip to some places can cost a small fortune but there are still some cheaper outings worth considering:

Local pantomimes, especially ones staged by an amateur company, can often be more fun than professional pantos. Apart from being caught up in the enthusiasm of the players, part of the fun for the children is spotting the milkman and the lollipop lady amongst the cast.

If you are lucky enough to be near an English Heritage or National Trust property, why not contact them to see if they have any activities taking place during the holiday? 'Living history' events can provide enough stimulation to keep children occupied even after the event.

Contact your local arts centre to see what performing arts and exhibitions they have planned for the festive season.

Your local library will have information about all events within your area and may even have their own children's activities running through Christmas and New Year.

Of course, it goes almost without saying: how about visiting Father Christmas in your local town?

Is there a circus coming to town this December?

Contact your local Tourist Information Centre to see if there are any local festivals over Christmas.

Sports and leisure centres will be running courses and clubs for children over the school holidays. Perhaps now could be the time for your children to learn to swim or take up in-line skating?

🎁 Does your nearest theatre run a children's workshop?

🎁 Dancing and music schools often run holiday courses – perfect for using up all that excess energy.

🎁 What are the local Brownie, Cub and Scout packs up to this holiday?

🎁 Beg, buy, or borrow a copy of *Kids' Britain* by Betty Jarman (published by Macmillan). It's an indispensible guide for parents giving ideas of places to visit, many of them with free admission, all over Great Britain and Northern Ireland.

PRESENT IDEAS FOR THE UNDER FIVES

Knowing what to buy small children if you don't have any of your own, can be fraught with difficulty. So, as the mother of two young children, I thought I'd give you a few pointers towards present ideas for fives and under. The first thing to remember about the very young is that they will almost certainly enjoy the wrapping paper as much as the contents – so you might as well please the parents by giving something useful. And, whatever age of child you are buying for, avoid any toys that require umpteen batteries and go 'beep beep' to the point at which an adult's frayed nerves are ... completely severed! The ideas I give here are for toys and games that I have seen my own – and friends' – children play with again and again.

FOR BABIES AND TODDLERS

Nowadays, the range of colourful, durable plastic toys for babies and toddlers is fantastic. Well-made wooden ones are well worth looking out for as they also last well. These toys will encourage hand-eye coordination and many of them are not too expensive.

🎁 No baby can have too many bibs so these are always welcomed as gifts by parents. You can get wipeable ones with vinyl shapes, like fish or birds, floating in between the clear front and back. They are fun and practical.

🎁 Cloth books are good for encouraging the reading habit. Plastic bath books are tough and waterproof for energetic bathtimes – you can even get song books for watery singalongs.

🎁 Decorative items for the nursery, like wallcharts and friezes, are available with all sorts of popular themes: the alphabet, colours, farm animals and licensed characters from popular books and films.

🎁 Still in the nursery, nightlights are available at prices to suit all pockets.

Nightlights are a boon for the many children who are afraid of the dark.

👜 Once a toddler is in a bed of his own, a very popular present is a small torch. You can get fun ones in animal shapes which you have to squeeze to light up. (The batteries in these are safely secured behind a Philip's head screw so they are quite safe for the younger toddler.) Or how about a simple pen torch that doesn't need expensive batteries? (These are best saved for older children who know not to play with batteries.)

FOR TODDLERS AND UP TO FIVE

If you have grandchildren or nieces and nephews who have to endure a long car journey to visit relatives, why not give them a story cassette tape? These are often sold in a gift pack with an accompanying book and are great for providing in-car entertainment or even for quietening down children after a boisterous game when you may not have time to read them a story yourself. My own family's favourites are the *Percy the Parkeeper* series by Nick Butterworth, *Alfie and Annie Rose* by Shirley Hughes and anything by Roald Dahl.

👜 I don't think you can beat the old-fashioned farm set which you can add and add to as the child grows up. Relatives who then ask for ideas for birthdays can be steered towards contributing flocks of sheep, combine harvesters, horse boxes and stables as the farm expands and diversifies!

👜 Felt picture games come in a hundreds of different varieties. They are cheap and provide hours of absorbed amusement.

👜 Plastic marble runs are tremendous and great for the imagination as you can expand the gift with extra sections to make whole rollercoaster runs for marbles to cascade at great speed.

👜 Any good-quality model and building games will get almost daily use. Duplo, Lego and K'NEX are all good investments and are equally popular with boys and girls. It may seem like you're playing safe with a gift like this but, honestly, these will be the toys that children return to over and over again. They also make excellent presents to send overseas: not only are they light and unlikely to get damaged in the post, but they can be bought in most countries – so you'd be sending something they could add to themselves.

👜 Well-designed craft kits will get children started on all sorts of artistic projects. Stencil packs give them the chance to incorporate exotic birds, butterflies and wild animals in their own pictures and paintings. Cross-stitch kits teach the rudiments of sewing. Bead sets come in all sorts of guises: from jewellery kits to boards for creating bead pictures.

🎁 Dressing-up accessories provide good props for home-produced plays. There are play tabards with matching hats that will turn infants into fire fighters, police officers, doctors, nurses and paramedics. Face paints provide hours of fun - but always make sure that you buy a reputable hypo-allergenic brand to make sure that, afterwards, faces really can be washed clean safely.

🎁 For stocking fillers, consider bubble guns which are hi-tech versions of the traditional wand-and-bubbles. Or how about drinking straws in bendy plastic that come in squirly-whirly shapes and even in the form of spectacles so that the soft drink whizzes round your eyes before going down your throat.

🎁 And finally, if you're feeling indulgent and want to splash out on a present you know will please a child around the age of five: a camera, a personal stereo, or a mini child's learning computer - any of these and you won't go far wrong.

BUY WITH CARE AND CAUTION

It may be tempting to buy a bargain in a street market or cut-price shop, but only buy toys if you are absolutely certain of their safety. There are currently three ways of checking that toys meet acceptable standards:

CE All toys sold in the UK have to conform to the Toy Safety Regulations, which interpret European rules and carry the CE mark.

British Standard 5665 Toys made in the UK should carry this mark on their packaging or the toy's label.

Lion Mark This is a safety mark for consumers, developed by the British Toy and Hobby Association. Look for the Lion Mark on display in good toy shops and on toys themselves.

COOKING WITH CHILDREN AT CHRISTMAS

I have never met a child who didn't enjoy cooking. I suspect that the licking-out of the bowl might have something to do with it but I also like to think that so does the magic of mixing all those ingredients so that something quite different emerges at the end. As little people might slow you down a touch with some of the more fiddly preparations, I've included some recipes here that are simple enough for children to cook with minimum supervision. Have fun – and don't forget to make them wash up!

CHOCOLATE AND APRICOT FLAPJACKS

INGREDIENTS

150 g (5 oz) soft margarine
150 g (5 oz) light muscovado sugar
225 g (8 oz) rolled oats
50 g (2 oz) ready-to-eat apricots, chopped into small pieces
25 g (1 oz) cooking chocolate drops

YOU WILL NEED

mixing bowl
flat baking tray, well greased

HERE THOSE *perennial favourites of chocolate and flapjacks make an irresistible combination.*

PRE-HEAT THE OVEN TO 350°F/180°C/GAS 4.

In a mixing bowl, beat together the sugar and margarine. Add the remaining ingredients and mix together well. Divide the mixture into small balls and press each of these gently on to the baking tray. Bake in the pre-heated oven for about 15 minutes until the biscuits are golden brown. Leave them on the baking tray to cool before removing them carefully with the spatula.

CHERRY AND ALMOND FINGERS

MAKES 16 FINGERS

INGREDIENTS

FOR THE BASE
75 g (3 oz) plain flour
25 g (1 oz) sugar
50 g (2 oz) soft margarine

FOR THE MIDDLE
75 g (3 oz) glacé cherries,
  cut into quarters
25 g (1 oz) sultanas

FOR THE TOP
50 g (2 oz) unsalted butter
50 g (2 oz) caster sugar
50 g (2 oz) ground
  almonds
1 large egg

YOU WILL NEED

20 cm (8 in) square
  cake tin
silicone paper or baking
  parchment
2 mixing bowls

THESE THREE-LAYER *biscuits would make a good present for a grandparent.*

PRE-HEAT THE OVEN TO 375°F/190°C/GAS 5. LINE THE BASE OF THE CAKE TIN WITH THE SILICONE PAPER OR BAKING PARCHMENT.

Place the ingredients for the base in a mixing bowl and rub them together lightly with your fingertips to form a dough. Press the dough down into the base of the cake tin. Sprinkle the dough with the cherries and the sultanas.

In a clean mixing bowl, mix together all the ingredients for the topping. When it is smooth and creamy, spread it on top of the fruit. Now place the cake tin in the centre of the pre-heated oven and bake for about 40 minutes until firm to the touch in the centre.

Remove the tin from the oven and allow it to cool thoroughly before cutting into 16 fingers.

CHOCOLATE BROWNIES

MAKES 15 BROWNIES

INGREDIENTS

FOR THE BROWNIES
100 g (4 oz) self-raising flour
¼ teaspoon salt
40 g (1½ oz) cocoa
100 g (4 oz) unsalted butter, softened
225 g (8 oz) soft dark brown or muscovado sugar
2 large eggs, beaten
1 tablespoon milk

FOR THE ICING
40 g (1½ oz) butter, melted
25 g (1 oz) cocoa, sieved
3 tablespoons evaporated milk
100 g (4 oz) icing sugar, sieved

YOU WILL NEED

28 x 18 x 2.5 cm (11 x 7 x 1 in) oblong baking tin
silicone paper or baking parchment
2 mixing bowls
sieve
pan

D ON'T FORGET *that these are meant to be squidgy in the middle.*

PRE-HEAT THE OVEN TO 375°F/190°C/GAS 5. GREASE AND LINE THE BAKING TIN WITH THE SILICONE PAPER OR BAKING PARCHMENT.

In a mixing bowl, sieve together the flour, salt and cocoa. In a separate bowl, beat together the butter and sugar until light and creamy. Add the eggs a little at a time, beating well in between. Fold the dry ingredients into this wet mixture along with the milk. Mix everything well before pouring it into the tin. Bake in the oven for about 30–35 minutes until the centre of the sponge springs back when pressed lightly. Allow the brownies to cool completely in the tin.

Make the icing by mixing the melted butter with the sieved cocoa in a pan. Cook over a low heat for about a minute. Remove the pan from the heat before adding the evaporated milk and the sieved icing sugar. Mix everything thoroughly and then spread the icing over the cooled brownies. Leave the icing to set before cutting into 15 squares.

PARTIES

PARTY PREPARATION

There is no better excuse than the festive season to hold a party. Whether you are holding a small drinks party or a larger hooley, planning ahead is the key to success, and will give you a chance of actually being able to mix with your guests and enjoy the evening as well. Thinking about some of the parties I've hosted myself (and the things I forgot to buy and do!) helped me to prepare this list of things to remember. I hope you will find it useful when planning a party of your own:

How many are you catering for? Do you have enough chairs if people need to sit down to eat?

Are you mixing children with adults? If so, consider the catering implications for the differing age groups as well as the best time of day to hold the event.

If you are inviting children, make sure that you don't serve peanuts, which are potentially dangerous as a choking hazard to young children in particular. In fact, bearing in mind the people suffering from peanut allergy these days, serve peanuts with caution what ever age your guests. (See page 67.)

Do you have enough crockery and cutlery? If not, can you borrow or hire some? (Look in your local paper or the Yellow Pages for catering suppliers.)

Set your budget before you get too far down the line. This will help you to decide what food and booze to select. (Chris Walker's party food recipes can be found on page 122 and Pat Chapman has some party ideas on page 60. For advice on drinks, refer to Martin Ward's wine tips on page 68.)

Will you have any help with the cooking and shopping? Can you do it on the day before the party?

Will you be serving food from a buffet-style table? In which case, do you have a table cloth to protect the table top? (Make sure it isn't too long, as you don't want your guests tripping over it.)

If you are presenting the food on one table for guests to help themselves from, make sure that you position everything within reach. If necessary, divide the food into portions and distribute it among a number of plates that can be strategically positioned along the table to allow good access.

🎀 Napkins are an essential, even if you are serving finger food and not having individual plates. It goes almost without saying that pretty, festive paper ones will save on the hard work afterwards.

🎀 Consider having a smaller table for the crockery and plates that your guests visit first. Then they will already have a plate to pile their food onto and it will also keep your guests moving, rather than congesting the buffet table area.

🎀 If you are serving food waitress-style during the party, will you need help to do this?

🎀 Make sure that you warn guests of any food that is piping hot as you serve it. You don't want them to go away only with memories of a burnt tongue!

🎀 Is your fridge big enough to hold all of the food? Can you ask a neighbour to accommodate anything that doesn't fit in your refrigerator? (Consult Fiona Hunter's kitchen hygiene advice on page 64 for guidance on preparing and storing food.)

🎀 Do you have enough glasses? Your local off-licence will certainly, given enough warning, be able to help with glass hire, and it's sometimes free if you buy the alcohol from them. Some supermarkets also provide this service.

🎀 Are you serving a selection of drinks or sticking to one drink, such as a punch, throughout the event? Do you need ice cubes? If so, either make this up with the disposable ice cube bags available from supermarkets or buy bags of ice from the supermarket, off-licence or a freezer-food shop.

🎀 Don't forget to have a selection of soft, non-alcoholic drinks available for those who prefer them, and for drivers.

🎀 Freeze slices of lemon ahead - see page 8 for advice on how to do this.

🎀 A clean, empty dustbin filled with ice or very cold water will serve as an excellent store for white wine, bottled water and soft drinks. Just make sure that you have enough tea-towels to wrap the bottles in or wipe the bottles with when they are removed from the dustbin.

🎀 Are you decorating the house with flowers for the party? Stephanie Donaldson's ideas on page 82 may be helpful to you. Or place an order with a local florist well ahead of the Christmas rush to avoid disappointment.

🎀 Be cautious with candles! They may look pretty, but can you keep enough of an eye on them during the evening to make sure they are safe?

✤ Make the house aromatic with Stephanie Donaldson's scented ideas on pages 104–106.

✤ What about music? Select your CDs and tapes well ahead of the event and, if possible, set up your music centre to play on a continuous loop so that you don't have to worry about the background music coming to a stop mid-evening. Decide on the level of the volume you want. If you are hoping your guests are going to mix, very loud music will prevent them from talking and will probably push the party out into the hall and stairs.

✤ Are you going to be playing any of the party games on pages 119–121? If so, get together all the props you'll need.

✤ How are you going to invite people to the event? By phone or with formal or informal invitations sent by post? There are so many attractive party invitations available from stationers and card shops these days that you may be spoilt for choice. Or, if you or a member of your family is a computer whizz, why not do your own?

✤ Winter parties mean that guests will almost certainly arrive in a thick woolly coat over their party clothes. Have you got someone who will be happy to take coats from guests as they arrive? (This is a great job to give to children.) And where are they going to put them?

✤ Get the loo ready for all those extra visitors! Make sure that you've got plenty of loo paper where people can find it. If you've really got a lot of guests coming, do you need to make a sign telling them where to go?

✤ Have you invited your neighbours to the party? Do you need to warn them about the potential noise and the extra cars?

✤ However polite your guests, with lots of people around accidents do happen. Have a dustpan and brush close to hand, as well as a clean cloth and stain salts for soaking up any wine and food spills.

✤ If you are not a smoker and are going to have smokers in the house, don't forget the ashtrays and a 'smokers' candle' to burn away the smells the next day.

✤ Have a local mini-cab firm's number near to the phone so that guests who need to can easily arrange their transport home.

✤ And finally, you might need listener Brian Turner's recipe for a hangover cure, which can be found on page 55.

PARTY GAMES

In the office, when we were thinking of ideas for parties, we all fondly remembered the parlour games of our childhood. I mentioned this on the programme one day and was especially delighted when Dee and James Ruppert from Norfolk wrote in to tell us of a number of traditional parlour games dating from at least the earlier part of this century. Judith Robertson from London also sent us some ideas that are included here. All the games are good old-fashioned fun - and could be another great way of keeping the children occupied in the build-up to Christmas. Why not play a few of them with your adult and family party guests?

THE ORACLE

Players gather around a radio (ideally tuned to BBC Radio 2, of course), turn down the sound, and ask the 'oracle' questions - the more ridiculous the better. The radio should then be turned up to answer in a suitably inappropriate, and therefore amusing, way.

SOUNDS

Someone goes behind a screen or door and makes various sounds: for instance, striking a match, cleaning shoes, folding a newspaper, and so on. The players have to guess what sound is being made, the more specifically the better - such as 'folding a copy of *Radio Times*'.

HUNT THE FEATHER

You need at least half-a-dozen players for this one, each sitting on chairs. Between all but one of them they hold out a sheet that is stretched out flat and on it is a feather. The one player not holding the sheet attempts to grab the feather whilst the others blow it out of reach. When the feather is caught, the player nearest the catcher gives up their seat and the game goes on ...

LEMON GOLF

For this you need walking sticks and lemons (one of each for each player). Place circular pieces of paper on the floor as the 'holes'. The winner is the player to get around the 'course' with the fewest strokes.

NB Be careful if children are playing this game - ornaments and heads are at risk from swinging walking sticks!

ORANGE BATTLE

This can either be played with oranges or tennis balls. Each player has two dessert spoons, one in each hand. In the left hand spoon is balanced an orange, the right hand spoon is used as a weapon against your opponents. If you drop an orange you are out and the last player with an orange still in the spoon wins.

LONG DISTANCE FLIGHT

Place a map of the world on the wall and cut out a photograph of an aircraft from a magazine, putting a loop of Sellotape on its back. Each player is blindfolded and walks to the map from the other side of the room to place the aircraft on the map. The player who 'travels' the furthest distance is the winner. You can also play this game with a map of the UK and a picture of a hitch-hiker instead of an aircraft - which can be quite amusing when the hitch-hiker ends up in the Irish Sea.

PLUM, PLUM, PLUM

You need between four and 12 people for this game. One person stands in the centre of a circle of people who are sitting down. Everyone chooses the name of a fruit for themselves and tells everyone what it is. Kumquat is a great favourite - the reason for this will become obvious.

The person in the middle has to say the name of one of the chosen fruits three times; they say, for instance, 'Pineapple, pineapple, pineapple.' The person who has chosen to be the Pineapple has to say the word once before, 'Pineapple,' is said by the centre player for the third time.

If Pineapple isn't concentrating, and doesn't say it in time, they have to stand up and replace the centre player who sits in their place and becomes Pineapple. So, every time the person in the centre wins, they sit in the seat of the person who wasn't concentrating and become that fruit. You may start as an Orange and end up a Kumquat - and try saying that three times quickly after a large Christmas lunch!

DING DONG (ALSO KNOWN AS KNIFE AND FORK)

This is a good one for playing immediately after a meal. The players sit round a table and one of them (A) starts off the game by taking his fork and, turning to the person on his left, says:

A: This is a Ding.
B: A what?
A: A Ding.
And on this, the fork changes hands. Player B turns to the player on his left and says:
B: This is a Ding.
C: A what?
B (turning back to A): A what?
A: A Ding.
B (to C):   A Ding.
C (taking the fork and turning to his left):   This is a Ding.
And so on round the circle. As soon as A has passed along the fork/Ding, he passes a knife (also known in this game as a Dong) in the opposite direction, with the dialogue proceeding in a similar fashion to that above only this time for a dong.

As you can imagine, the whole thing gets terribly confusing (and amusing) when Ding meets Dong.

PICTURE CONSEQUENCES

For this you'll need sheets of plain paper and as many pencils as there are players. The first player draws the head of an animal, folds the paper so that only the edge of the neck is visible, and passes it on. The second player draws the torso, folds and passes on, and the third draws the legs. Then the consequence is revealed to all. A great game for children and their family.

POETRY CONSEQUENCES

Again, you'll need paper, this time lined, and pencils. A first line of poetry is chosen by all the players, say, 'My love is like a red, red rose', and each player heads his paper with it.

Each player then supplies his own second line, say, 'And with her thorns she sits and sews' and a third as well, to begin the second couplet, say, 'Poppers on my anorak'. The paper should then be folded to show only the last line and is then passed on. The next player completes the couplet and begins a new one, folding the paper over to hide all but his last line before passing it on.

Keep on going until the paper is finished and then read the various poems aloud. You have to have your wits about you for this one!

PARTY NIBBLES

When we were thinking of all the things you have to remember when you throw a party, the one thing all of us who work on the programme had on our individual lists was 'party food'. We all agreed that some of the ready-prepared party food that is available in supermarkets is excellent, but that nothing beats something scrumptious and home made. So we had a word with our friend Chris Walker (of the Radio 2 Christmas Truffle Collection fame, see page 51) and asked him if he could come up with some ideas. We gave him a strict brief: the food had to be quick to prepare, quite delicious, easy to eat with your fingers, and some of the recipes had to be suitable for vegetarians. Here are the five recipes that Chris came up with. We think you'll agree that your party guests are in for a treat!

BRUSHETTA BREAD

INGREDIENTS

1 freshly baked white bloomer
2 teaspoons pesto (you can buy this ready-made in good supermarkets)
1 teaspoons tomato purée
25 g (1 oz) ground almonds
2 tablespoons olive oil
a few fresh mixed herbs, finely chopped

YOU WILL NEED

mixing bowl
baking tray

THIS IS ONE *of my favourite recipes, and it is so simple. Eat it as it is or lay thin slices of smoked salmon over it and finish off with a knob of fromage frais.*

PRE-HEAT THE OVEN TO 300°F/150°C/GAS 2.

First slice your bloomer into thicknesses that suit you. In a bowl, mix the pesto, tomato purée and the ground almonds. Dowse the bloomer generously in olive oil and then spread the pesto mixture over the bread. Sprinkle each slice with the herbs and lightly bake them in the pre-heated oven for about 10 minutes.

Once you get the hang of them you can make all sorts of additions to brushetta: perhaps some crushed garlic, or freshly ground black pepper, or olives or ... use your imagination!

PRAWN AND ASPARAGUS FILO PARCELS

MAKES 16 PARCELS

INGREDIENTS

2 tablespoons olive oil
½ onion, finely chopped
1 large tin of asparagus
spears, well drained and
chopped
1 leaf of fresh basil, finely
chopped
1 teaspoon tomato purée
175 g (6 oz) prawns
1 teaspoon double cream
8 sheets of filo pastry (buy
this frozen in most good
supermarkets)
50 g (2 oz) butter, melted

YOU WILL NEED

pan
pastry brush
baking tray, buttered

THESE LOOK REALLY *good: piping-hot, crispy, filo-pastry bite-sized parcels filled with prawns and asparagus. The parcels can be made in advance up to the ready-to-cook stage, if you prefer. If you decide to do that, make sure that you wrap the parcels well in cling film - filo pastry dries out very quickly if left open to the air. Make a lot of them as they disappear quickly!*

PRE-HEAT THE OVEN TO 425°F/220°C/GAS 7.

Heat the olive oil in the pan and gently sauté the chopped onion and asparagus spears. Allow the onion to brown and then add the basil and tomato purée. Add the prawns and then stir in the cream. Allow the mixture to thicken and then set it aside to cool.

When you are ready, lay a sheet of filo pastry on a work surface and brush it with the melted butter. Cover the pastry with the second sheet of filo and brush it with butter again. Cut the double sheets in half lengthways and then again widthways. Put a spoonful of the cooled filling in the centre of each square and fold the edges inward to make a parcel. Brush each parcel with melted butter and put them on the buttered baking tray.

Cook the parcels for about 7-10 minutes or until the pastry is golden and crisp. Don't forget to warn your guests that the parcels are hot before they bite into them!

SHERRY-LEMON CHICKEN DRUMSTICKS

SERVES 6

INGREDIENTS

25 g (1 oz) plain flour
4 tablespoons fresh thyme,
 finely chopped
1 ½ teaspoons dried thyme
6 fresh chicken drumsticks
2 ½ teaspoons olive oil
150 ml (6 fl oz) good
 chicken stock
1 tablespoon fresh lemon
 juice
50 ml (2 fl oz) dry sherry
1 garlic clove, crushed

YOU WILL NEED

mixing bowl
non-stick heavy-based frying
 pan
baking tray or roasting tin

A REALLY TASTY *idea to brighten up chicken drumsticks for party nibbles.*

PRE-HEAT THE OVEN TO 400°F/200°C/GAS 6.

In a bowl, mix the flour with the fresh thyme and 1 teaspoon of the dried thyme. Coat each of the chicken drumsticks in the flour mixture, shaking off the excess. Heat 2 teaspoons of the olive oil in the frying pan, add the drumsticks and brown them on all sides.

Place the drumsticks on the roasting tray and cook them in the oven for about 15 minutes, turning them half-way through the cooking time.

Meanwhile, in the same frying pan, add the remaining olive oil and heat this before adding the stock, lemon juice, sherry and garlic and stir very thoroughly. Bring the mixture to the boil and then add the remaining fresh thyme, stirring. Simmer until the sauce thickens and then either pour the sauce over the drumsticks or serve as a hot dip.

YOGHURT AND FETA CHEESE DIP

INGREDIENTS

250 ml (8 fl oz) natural
yoghurt (I prefer to use
Greek or Greek-style)
100 g (4 oz) feta cheese,
crumbled
1 large onion, roughly
chopped
¼ teaspoon finely grated
lemon zest
freshly ground black pepper

YOU WILL NEED

food processor

THIS IS IDEAL to serve with crudités. It can be made up to two days ahead as long as you keep it covered and chilled in the refrigerator.

Place all the ingredients into the food processor and purée until smooth. Season with pepper and chill for at least 2 hours until cold.

SWEET PICKLED HERRING WITH CUCUMBER AND DILL CRÉME FRAÎCHE

INGREDIENTS

½ cucumber
about 12 sweet pickled
herring fillets
handful of fresh dill,
finely chopped
200 ml (7 fl oz) créme
fraîche

YOU WILL NEED

cocktail sticks
serving bowl and plate

SWEET PICKLED herrings are now readily available in most large supermarkets. In this recipe I have added cucumber to them to give this particular nibble a 'crunch'.

Peel the cucumber and then cut it into chunks. Place a chunk in the centre of each herring fillet and wrap the fillet around the cucumber. Take a cocktail stick and skewer the herring and cucumber securely into place. Mix the dill into the créme fraîche. Serve as a dip for the herring or carefully place a teaspoon of the mixture onto each herring.

A CHRISTMAS WEEK COUNTDOWN

In our house, this is when the excitement really begins to set in. I find endless list-making helps me feel more at ease, and these tips are based on my own family's ideas and those of my colleagues.

A WEEK BEFORE

If you usually cut into your cake on Christmas Eve, you should really cover the cake with almond icing about a week before. Follow Mary Berry's advice on page 12 and then leave it for a few days to dry out before you do the royal or fondant icing.

Do most of your food shopping, freezing perishables such as cream and butter. (As you unpack the shopping work out, with the help of other family members, what you have forgotten.)

Post any last-minute Christmas cards and presents now if you haven't already before it's too late.

Buy and decorate your tree and start decking the halls with boughs of holly.

Check with your butcher or supplier when you should collect your turkey.

If possible, order the fruit and vegetables you will need from your supplier, ready to collect on Christmas Eve.

Fill in your emergency names and numbers (see page 141).

FIVE DAYS BEFORE

Ice and decorate your cake according to Mary Berry's guidance – see page 14.

Start making your mince pies.

You could make your brandy butter now and freeze it.

THREE DAYS BEFORE

Start making Chris Walker's Radio 2 Christmas Truffle Collection if you are planning to eat these on Christmas Eve and Christmas Day.

Have you delivered all your local cards and presents by hand? Do it now!

TWO DAYS BEFORE

If you are having a frozen bird, start to thaw the turkey now (see Fiona Hunter's advice on page 64).

🕊 As I mentioned before, I prefer to use a fresh bird, which allows me to use the giblets to make my giblet stock gravy now (see page 25).
🕊 Run through the Christmas reminder list on page 128. Have you forgotten anything?

CHRISTMAS EVE

MORNING & AFTERNOON

Now is really the time to do any last-minute food shopping. If you can, buy and collect your fruit and vegetables today so that they will be in optimum condition.
🕊 Check the weight of your turkey and decide what time you are going to sit down to eat tomorrow. Combine the two to work out when the cooking process should begin in earnest.
🕊 Enrol any help you can get to prepare the vegetables for cooking tomorrow. You can at least wash and slice some of them and set aside in the refrigerator now, or place in a covered saucepan of water.

EVENING

Make the stuffing for the turkey - see the recipes on pages 22 and 24.
🕊 Make the bread sauce (see recipe on page 34) and set aside, covered and away from the heat, ready to re-heat tomorrow.

🕊 Following your family traditions, do Santa's job by delivering the presents around the tree or in pillow cases.
🕊 Put out any stockings by bedsides.
🕊 Try to get a good night's sleep.

CHRISTMAS DAY

MORNING

Stuff the bird (see pages 24 and 65).
🕊 Start roasting your turkey according the time that you are aiming to sit down, checking it periodically to ensure that it is OK.
🕊 Time the cooking of the vegetables.
🕊 Remember to warm the plates!
🕊 Delegate the table-laying to someone else if you can - but don't forgot to include Stephanie Donaldson's gorgeous table decorations in the plan (see page 88). Don't forget the napkins and the crackers.
🕊 Prepare the bacon rolls ready for cooking according to your deadline.
🕊 Start simmering your Byre Farm Christmas Pudding (see page 17) about one hour before you think you will sit down to eat it.
🕊 Open and decant or chill your wine according to Martin Ward's advice (see pages 68-71).

LUNCH TIME

Sit down and enjoy your meal and the rest of your day!

THE ULTIMATE CHRISTMAS REMINDER LIST

There are so many things to remember to have close at hand at this time of year. So, having gone through all our experts' advice, and thinking of my own and my colleagues experiences, here is a comprehensive list of general items you'll need in the house at Christmas. Add your own family's special needs at the end.

☐ Quiche tins

☐ Roasting tins

☐ Cake tins

☐ Pudding basin

☐ Mixing bowls and dishes

☐ Cakeboard

☐ Cake storage tin

☐ Cake decorations

☐ Muslin (see turkey recipe on page 22)

☐ Cling film

☐ Greaseproof paper, silicone paper, or baking parchment

☐ Turkey-sized foil

☐ Sticky tape

☐ Batteries

☐ Wrapping paper

☐ Scissors

☐ Cards

☐ Gift tags

☐ Party invitations

☐ String

☐ Spare pads (for all the party games on page 119)

☐ Pens and pencils

☐ Crackers

☐ Napkins

☐ Tablecloths

☐ Tea towels

☐ Washing-up brush

☐ Cleaning cloths

☐ Disinfectant

☐ Washing-up liquid

☐ Washing powder (you may need extra if there are lots of people staying over the holiday)

☐ Stain removers and stain salts

☐ Fridge thermometer (see Fiona Hunter's advice on page 66)

☐ Ice-cube trays or bags

☐ Cocktail sticks

☐ Paper sweet cases

☐ Cocktail decorations

☐ Nappies

☐ Baby formula milk and food

☐ General baby and toddler items (if you have a grandchild or young relation staying for Christmas it may be possible for you to borrow a cot or high-chair from a friend to save the child's parents from bring-ing very large items with them. Alternatively, contact your local child health clinic and ask them if they know of any local agency that may hire out such items, or consult *The Good Deal Directory* by Noelle Walsh, which lists such agencies by region (telephone 01367 860016 for details of how to obtain a copy).

☐ Pet supplies

☐ Nut crackers ... or two!

☐ Candles

☐ Emergency presents

☐ Extra crockery and cutlery

☐ Items that may make life easier for elderly guests (if you have a relative who normally lives in a home or sheltered housing stay-ing for the holiday, ask the home if they can lend items such as special cups, lavatory and bath seats, and wheelchairs if they are necessary to help make life more comfortable. Or contact your local health authority or Help the Aged office to enquire about local agencies that may be able to provide such a service.)

☐ Decorations

☐ Christmas tree (see Adam Pasco's advice on page 78)

☐ Tree lights and spare bulbs

☐ Tree decorations

☐ Writing paper and envelopes (for all those thank-you letters!)

☐ Extra bed linen (if you have guests staying)

☐ Sleeping bags (for younger or heartier guests!)

☐ Dustbin bags

CHRISTMAS FOOD & DRINK LIST

Your own family will have Christmas food favourites and many of the ingredients used in our wonderful Christmas recipes may well be found in your kitchen cupboards anyway. Here is a list of things that you will want to consider having in store for festive cookery:

DAIRY PRODUCE

- ☐ Milk
- ☐ Cream, single and double
- ☐ Butter
- ☐ Créme Fraîche
- ☐ Yoghurt
- ☐ Eggs

MEAT

- ☐ Turkey
- ☐ Ham
- ☐ Beef
- ☐ Bacon
- ☐ Sausages
- ☐ Sausagemeat

FRIDGE AND FREEZER FOODS

- ☐ Christmas pudding (to make your own, see Mary Berry's recipe on page 17)
- ☐ Frozen pastry, shortcrust, flaky and filo
- ☐ Brandy cream or sauce (to make your own, see the recipe suggestions on pages 17 and 36)
- ☐ Ice cubes
- ☐ Ice-cream (see Mary Berry's Christmas Brandy Ice-cream Pudding recipe on page 18)

FRUIT

- ☐ Apples
- ☐ Pears
- ☐ Oranges
- ☐ Satsumas
- ☐ Clementines
- ☐ Lemons (see freezer tip on page 8)
- ☐ Limes
- ☐ Pineapple (see Stephanie Donaldson's table suggestions on page 88)
- ☐ Grapes

- ☐ Kiwi fruit
- ☐ Bananas

VEGETABLES

- ☐ Potatoes
- ☐ Parsnips
- ☐ Brussels sprouts
- ☐ Onions
- ☐ Celery
- ☐ Garlic
- ☐ Carrots

GENERAL LARDER ITEMS

- ☐ Cranberry sauce
- ☐ Mincemeat (see the home-made recipe idea on page 48)
- ☐ Nuts, in their shells and for cookery: almonds, pecans, brazils, hazelnuts
- ☐ Vegetable oil
- ☐ Olive oil
- ☐ Baking powder
- ☐ Tea
- ☐ Coffee
- ☐ Cocoa powder
- ☐ Sugar: soft brown, muscovado, granulated, caster, icing
- ☐ Flour: plain and self-raising
- ☐ Sage-and-onion stuffing mix
- ☐ Candied peel
- ☐ Dried fruits for cakes: mixed peel, currants, raisins, sultanas
- ☐ Pickles

- ☐ Chocolates and chocolate for cookery
- ☐ Crisps and snacks
- ☐ Sweet biscuits
- ☐ Bread
- ☐ Biscuits for cheese
- ☐ Stock cubes
- ☐ Salt and pepper
- ☐ Herbs and spices
- ☐ Pet food
- ☐ Pasta
- ☐ Rice

DRINKS

- ☐ Red and white wine (see Martin Ward's advice on page 68)
- ☐ Champagne (again, see page 68 for Martin Ward's guidance)
- ☐ Gin
- ☐ Whisky/whiskey
- ☐ Brandy
- ☐ Beer
- ☐ Cider
- ☐ Liqueurs and spirits
- ☐ Lemonade
- ☐ Cola
- ☐ Soda water
- ☐ Tonic water
- ☐ Ginger beer
- ☐ Ginger ale
- ☐ Orange juice
- ☐ Apple juice
- ☐ Grape juice
- ☐ Bottled water

CHRISTMAS CARD LIST

Christmas cards are a great way of keeping in touch with distant friends and loved ones. I really enjoy reading people's news and telling them about what my family has got up to during the previous year. But it seems that every year my list of people to send cards to gets longer and longer, and the only way I can keep tabs on who I've still to write to is by keeping a list. If you have the same problem as I do, I hope that you find this chart of use over the next few years to help keep you in control of the situation. Don't forget that each year the Royal Mail issues a leaflet giving details of last posting dates, which is essential for those of you who have friends and relations overseas as well as in the UK.

NAME	1997			1998			1999			2000		
	CARD SIGNED	CARD STAMPED	CARD POSTED	CARD SIGNED	CARD STAMPED	CARD POSTED	CARD SIGNED	CARD STAMPED	CARD POSTED	CARD SIGNED	CARD STAMPED	CARD POSTED

NAME	1997			1998			1999			2000		
	CARD SIGNED	CARD STAMPED	CARD POSTED	CARD SIGNED	CARD STAMPED	CARD POSTED	CARD SIGNED	CARD STAMPED	CARD POSTED	CARD SIGNED	CARD STAMPED	CARD POSTED

NAME	1997			1998			1999			2000		
	CARD SIGNED	CARD STAMPED	CARD POSTED	CARD SIGNED	CARD STAMPED	CARD POSTED	CARD SIGNED	CARD STAMPED	CARD POSTED	CARD SIGNED	CARD STAMPED	CARD POSTED

NAME	1997			1998			1999			2000		
	CARD SIGNED	CARD STAMPED	CARD POSTED	CARD SIGNED	CARD STAMPED	CARD POSTED	CARD SIGNED	CARD STAMPED	CARD POSTED	CARD SIGNED	CARD STAMPED	CARD POSTED

CHRISTMAS PRESENT LISTS

Despite the hard work of buying the presents it's actually great fun to choose the perfect gift for someone. But my great mistake is that I always leave the wrapping until the very last minute and then try to wrap everything in one fraught evening, only to discover that I haven't got enough gift tags and the dog has chewed half of the sticky tape! We were talking about this in the office last Christmas and decided that a Christmas present list was an essential to include in this book. So we pooled our thoughts and also came up with a list of things that you may want to have to hand when you start wrapping, as well as some guidelines for those of you who are putting presents in the post.

WRAPPING CHECKLIST

☐ Pens

☐ Gift tags

☐ Wrapping paper

☐ Bubble wrap, newspaper or shredded paper (to protect delicate items and pad out awkward shapes)

☐ Scissors

☐ String

☐ Christmas parcel ribbon

☐ sticky tape

☐ Something heavy (to hold down the paper while you wrestle with the other end of it)

☐ Cardboard boxes (especially if you are wrapping delicate items or putting things in the post)

☐ 'Fragile' stickers

☐ Padded posting bags (you can get these from the post office and good stationers)

☐ Large cardboard box or strong bin bag (for keeping the presents in when you've wrapped them)

POSTING AND PACKING TIPS

🎁 Books are best packed in padded envelopes, but make sure that the envelope isn't much bigger than the book. If it is, the book will move around in the envelope and its jacket will get damaged.

🎁 Seal the lids of tins or bottles with sticky tape and wrap each bottle in bubblewrap to protect them. Label the parcels as 'fragile'.

🎁 If you are giving house plants, see Adam Pasco's tips on page 72.

🎁 If you are giving someone a print or picture that isn't framed, sandwich the print between stiff cardboard that is larger than the picture itself. If the picture is framed, cover it in bubblewrap, or similar, before you put the top layer of wrapping paper on. Mark the parcel as 'fragile'.

🎁 If you are giving a perishable gift, remember that there are restrictions on sending such things by post. Ask your local post office for guidance - although, of course, if you are sending gifts direct from the manufacturer (see Sally O'Sullivan's brilliant Presents By Post ideas on page 89), there will not be a problem. Always make sure that you tell the recipient that the gift needs to be placed in the fridge or kept in a cool place.

🎁 Computer games and videos need special handling as they can be damaged or even wiped 'clean' if they come into contact with a magnetic field. You can buy special envelopes and boxes for posting computer discs (ask at a good stationers or a large post office), or tell the recipient to keep such a present away from things like a microwave oven (it can scramble the disk as well as eggs!).

🎁 Don't put batteries in toys before you wrap them. Sometimes the 'bleep' or action of the toy can be triggered if it is moved too often. This not only gives the game away (and drives pets wild) but will also wear down the batteries before necessary.

🎁 China and any delicate objects should be carefully protected with many layers of newspaper or bubblewrap and preferably placed in a box, secured into position with packing material, before the pretty layer of wrapping paper is finally applied. Don't forget to mark the gift tag 'fragile'.

🎁 Be careful with staples, which can cause nasty cuts when a present is being opened, especially by a child. Make sure that they are covered with a layer of protective sticky tape. (Look out for the boxes that toys are sold in, as many have staples. Toys manufactured in European countries will almost certainly be packaged safely to EC standards, but check them anyway.)

🎁 If the item you are posting is
irreplaceable, ask your post office for
advice before simply sending it off.
Recorded, special delivery and registered post are guaranteed services, so
ask which one you need.
🎁 Some items cannot be posted.
These may seem obvious but here
they are:
    Aerosols
    Asbestos
    Butane lighters and refills
    Compressed flammable gases
    Corrosives (including dyes)
    Counterfeit currency, bank notes
        and postage stamps
    Drugs prohibited for general use
        by law
    Dry ice
    Explosives (including Christmas
        crackers)
    Flammable liquids or solids
        (including adhesives)
    Indecent, obscene or offensive
        material
    Living creatures (some insects are
        exempt, though! Ask for
        guidance)

Matches of any kind
Oxidizing material and organic
    peroxide (such as disinfectants)
Paints and varnishes
Poisons
Radioactive materials (including
    pacemakers)
Sharp instruments
Toxic and other dangerous materials

🎁 The Royal Mail publishes various
helpful leaflets on packing and posting both in the UK and abroad. Ask
for these from your local post office.
🎁 If you are sending a gift abroad,
consider the weight and delicacy of
the item before you buy it. (I once
sent something that was so heavy the
postage cost more than the gift!) You
should also check the last posting
dates for the destination for both surface and airmail. Surface mail for
Australia, for example, might need to
be in the post by the beginning of
October in some years. Don't leave it
too late to take advantage of the
cheapest postal method - ask for
guidance at the post office.

CHRISTMAS PRESENT-WRAPPING LIST

YEAR	RECIPIENT	GIFT IDEA	WRAPPED	TAGGED	DELIVERED	POSTED
1997						
1998						
1999						
2000						
1997						
1998						
1999						
2000						
1997						
1998						
1999						
2000						
1997						
1998						
1999						
2000						
1997						
1998						
1999						
2000						

YEAR	RECIPIENT	GIFT IDEA	WRAPPED	TAGGED	DELIVERED	POSTED
1997						
1998						
1999						
2000						
1997						
1998						
1999						
2000						
1997						
1998						
1999						
2000						
1997						
1998						
1999						
2000						
1997						
1998						
1999						
2000						

EMERGENCY NAMES & NUMBERS

No one wants anything to go wrong at Christmas but, in case it does, it is best to be prepared so that the crisis can be resolved as quickly as possible. When those of us who work on the programme had one of our Christmas brainstorming sessions, we came up with the following ideas for names and numbers to have at hand – just in case:

Doctor	Local supermarket
Dentist	Local garage
Local accident and emergency	Local gas company
department	Local electricity company
Local chemist open	Local coal merchant/home fuel
over Christmas	company
Local police station	Local septic tank service
Vet	Plumber
Local shop	Electrician
Local bank	Glazier
Nearest cash machine	Motoring rescue service
located at	

Include here any other numbers that are relevant to your home and family:

INDEX